50 SHADES OF *Black and White*

An Idealist's Reflections

**Opening Boxes
Exploring Work, Life and Health
Options From the Grey Zone**

Petra Goerschel

First published by Ultimate World Publishing 2021
Copyright © 2021 Petra Georschel

ISBN

Paperback: 978-1-922597-63-2
Ebook: 978-1-922597-64-9

Petra Georschel has asserted her rights under the Copyright, Designs and Patents Act 1988 to be identified as the author of this work. The information in this book is based on the author's experiences and opinions. The publisher specifically disclaims responsibility for any adverse consequences which may result from use of the information contained herein. Permission to use information has been sought by the author. Any breaches will be rectified in further editions of the book.

All rights reserved. No part of this publication may be reproduced, stored in or introduced into a retrieval system, or transmitted in any form, or by any means (electronic, mechanical, photocopying, recording or otherwise) without the prior written permission of the author. Any person who does any unauthorised act in relation to this publication may be liable to criminal prosecution and civil claims for damages. Enquiries should be made through the publisher.

Cover design: Ultimate World Publishing
Layout and typesetting: Ultimate World Publishing
Editor: Isabelle Russell
Cover copyright image: Tongsai-Shutterstock.com

Ultimate World Publishing
Diamond Creek,
Victoria Australia 3089
www.writeabook.com.au

Acknowledgement

I would like to acknowledge all of the people who encouraged, supported and inspired me to continue with writing this book. So as not to miss anyone, I have not listed you individually, but I give my sincere thanks to each and every one of you.

Contents

Acknowledgement	iii
Introduction	1
1. Productivity Challenges—Punished for Doing Good	11
2. Policy and Procedures vs Trust	27
3. Local vs Global—Sustainability	37
4. People vs Profits—Values	49
5. Council Candidate	63
6. Social Media Impacts	81
7. Good Neighbours	87
8. Respecting Others	97
9. Balancing Priorities	105
10. Self-Care—Others—Me or We	113
11. Be a Good Friend—Notice Anger	125
12. Looking after the Future	135
Acknowledgement to Country	151
Declaration for Earth—Revoking Unconscious Consent	153
References	155
Speaker Bio	157
About the Author	160

Introduction

I have resigned from being part of the 'human experiment' and am rewiring myself and my life. This is the journey to reclaiming my life. The older I get, the more I realise how little I know. Whilst I have gained a lot of knowledge throughout my years, I have, more importantly, gained much more wisdom. In my youth, everything seemed much simpler, and, in many ways, it was. What I had learnt became my beliefs, and my beliefs on certain topics were either this way or that, right or wrong, black or white—definitely no room for grey. However, as I have gone through the changes of life, I have come to realise things are not always as they are portrayed to be. As we enquire further into the various aspects of humanity and our life as it is, some things no longer seem to add up.

The more technology is evolving, the less I want to be part of the evolution. I have found myself retreating more and more into a world that is not familiar to me. It feels like trying to fit a square peg into a round hole. This book began whilst I was trying to figure out 'why' and 'how to' live in a world that has become unrecognisable and uncomfortable.

For many years now, I have felt more and more like a product rather than a human being. It seems as though everyone wants my feedback and yet most times there is no 'tick box' for what I would like to say. I no longer answer my phone to numbers I am not familiar with due to the barrage of calls, texts or emails trying to ask or sell me something I don't want. At least with the old snail mail, there was a limit to how much contact we could have—and were subjected to.

Thank you to the person who recently triggered me so much, I found myself screaming at the television. The extreme anger and sheer frustration I felt towards the narrator who seemed to be 'aggressively demanding' that I do what she wanted me to do. What had just happened to me and why was I so triggered? Have any of you ever found yourself in a similar situation, screaming at the television, ranting on social media or directly venting your frustrations to another human being?

This was definitely my wake-up call and a mirror for me to look at what was happening in my life. I realised that I too have probably tried to 'aggressively demand' something of someone else at some point in my life. Gratefully, I have evolved and I recognise no-one has the right to 'demand' anything of anyone else. I have always been described as a serious thinker, and I have had a lot of time to ponder and reflect on life and the myriad changes that have occurred. For years, I have been told to write a book. So, I would like to share with you my personal reflections, experiences and beliefs, many of which have changed over time. This incident also reminded me that the overarching principle of what I wanted to achieve with this book was to do no harm and present this information in the best way I can.

What I have come to realise is there were many times in my life that I was given warnings about what was not good for me. However, most times, I took no notice and ignored the warnings. Looking back, I received many subtle warnings, the feather touch, which I ignored or was told to ignore, until I got the sledgehammer which stopped me in my tracks and made me take notice and respond in a different way to what I had previously done.

In my idealistic world I believe all things created by people should harm no one and be of benefit to everyone. However, in the real world that is not often the case. So, I started to question the changes I have observed both in business and in health. When money isn't your main motivation for doing business, then success has a very different meaning. Living in today's world is so much easier and better in many ways however not all is for the greater good. I am reminded of the natural life cycle of the butterfly and how it needs to struggle and grow through the chrysalis or pupa stage in order to emerge as a beautiful butterfly. Are the struggles humanity is currently experiencing required so that we can strengthen for our future evolution?

Looking back over my life, I realised from a very young age, the things that seem to work for others just did not work for me in the same way. However, throughout my life I still continued to try all of the various patches that were recommended by others from whom I sought counsel for my physical, emotional and social challenges. The problem with looking outside of myself for solutions was nobody really knew who I was and what I needed to make me tick efficiently. For that matter, neither did I. At the time, I valued the opinions and solutions offered by others as part of finding what was best for me. The gift in strange wrapping paper was the reflections that arose from the outer experiences, which showed me I was not on the right track for my life.

The work, for me, needed to start from within myself. I needed to find my own solutions. The challenge to this was stopping the distractions so I could go inside to unlock my sovereignty. I wonder if we are all on the same journey to find inner peace. A wise mentor once told me to read widely from many different sources and then narrow the information down to what best suits you and your lifestyle. With so much information freely available on the internet, this can be both a blessing and a curse. Sometimes it feels as though, as a society, we are being directed from independence to dependence, with the definition of independence being 'freedom from the control or influence of others.' Is independence even realistic in our modern world! It is often not until our freedoms have been restricted that we realise, or consciously question, what freedoms we have had, enjoyed, valued and appreciated. It has been said, we often don't realise what we have had until we lose it.

It took me fifty years to realise I had handed over my life to others on so many occasions in the never-ending search for a solution. Mind you, I have to admit, it is much easier going to someone else for the answer to my problem, because when things don't work out, then I can blame others for not 'fixing' my problem. On top of that I have been naive enough to expect, if a product is provided then it is safe.

Mirror, mirror on the wall, please help me to find the product and people that do no harm, act in a supportive, integrous, trustworthy and respectful manner, and of course would never act in a fraudulent, deceptive or dishonest manner in order to gain an advantage. These people and products do exist, however sometimes you have to dig a little deeper to find these diamonds. When I was bleeding, metaphorically speaking, the sharks circled. If this ever happens to you, do not feed the sharks.

The bottom line is, I don't know it all. A lot of healing can come from simply being listened to and being heard. The trick is trust yourself and stay out of fear, so you can clearly see what is in front of you and make wiser choices. Fear breeds and enhances any dis-ease whereas love and gratitude can conquer fear. Most of all, it is important to honour how we feel. We can only heal what we allow ourselves to feel. It is believed that the challenges we go through in life are actually good because they develop a latent strength within us that would not have developed without the challenges. When you change the way in which you see things from inside, then the things outside you seem to change.

In the process of writing this book, I have reflected on many areas of my life. The journey starts from pencil, pen and paper to being run by a computer. This was the evolution of the fifty-plus years of my working life. Whilst I have always enjoyed change, this with regard to technology, is no longer the case. The constant upgrade of computers and their programs, the additional learning and work required to train and support staff and the constant physical and emotional pressures to meet deadlines became impossible. There was no dedicated computer support department at the time, therefore pencil and paper were definitely easier and less stressful. No wonder I have not kept up with technology as those final years of work were horrendous.

The blessing of being literate is being able to become more educated. The more I read, the more I learn. Whilst I don't always believe everything I read, my intuition is my guide. In my reflections I have been drawn to the wisdom and knowledge of our ancestors and indigenous people. In many ways, I feel as though the humanity has left our societies whilst cyber interactions and the stuff of things have taken over. Be discerning and keep an open mind as the marketing these days is very persuasive and not necessarily truthful. If we adopt an overarching principle of 'do no harm' with everything we say, buy or do, and if every business considered this when producing all its products, the world would be a very different place. I am a dreamer who believes, when enough people with a similar mindset get together, change will occur. The Pachamama Alliance is a not-for-profit organisation that enshrines and aims to bridge the gap in the relationship between the 'developed' modern societies and the leaders of remote indigenous groups in the Amazon region of Ecuador. With their dream, I too, have envisioned a new dream for a human presence which is environmentally sustainable, spiritually fulfilling and for everyone.

We are living in a time where leadership can be so easily influenced and compromised. Taking personal responsibility and accountability seem to be just words with little or no corresponding actions. Having a conflict of interest seems to mean something different these days. In the past, CEOs of organisations were jailed if their company was found to be using deceptive marketing practices, downplaying the risks of their products and overstating and embellishing the benefits. Now, it seems like selling potentially harmful goods while concealing relevant information, denies potential customers the right to be fully informed before giving their consent. In these current times, this barely attracts a fine or even so much as a slap on the wrist by any of the regulatory authorities.

When is enough really enough? When I say no, I really do mean no. When I say I don't want something, I really don't want it. Most of all, I don't appreciate being coerced, bullied, bribed and manipulated into having what others want me to have. I have not given companies consent to upgrade my system, nor to put things on my computer that I did not ask for. So, do not automatically upgrade my computer or do anything without my approval. Bigger or upgraded does not equal better in my world. When the word 'inclusive' is being used, does that really include me? The world we live in at the moment feels like being on a runaway train and I want to get off at the next station. Everything is changing too fast and I am having trouble keeping up. I would like to be able to choose whether I want to come along or not. Not all change is for the greater good.

I would like to see a future where we deal with the cause and not the effect of our disease, create sustainable products made with materials that last, are repairable and recyclable. Maybe it is time to reconsider what our insatiable appetite for 'stuff' is creating and if it is really sustainable. What if humanity was able to heal the unresolved personal trauma's instead of using retail therapy, comfort eating, gambling and so on, as a band-aide or quick fix.

Introduction

The cynic in me believes some people are motivated purely by self-interest rather than acting for honourable or unselfish reasons. The idealist in me, knows it takes a lot of courage to speak up and speak out. So, if you have picked up this book then there is something in here for you. Enjoy.

'This new world should be the world in which the rich won't exploit the weak, the bad won't exploit the good, where the poor won't be humiliated by the rich. It will be the world in which the children of the intellect, science and skill, will serve the community in order to make lives easier and nicer. And not to the individuals for gaining wealth. This new world can't be the world of the humiliated, the broken, but the world of free people and nations equal in dignity and respect for man.'
Nikola Tesla

'Life is what happens to you while you're busy making other plans.'
John Lennon

1

Productivity Challenges— Punished for Doing Good

PRODUCTIVITY

> *'Change happens when the pain of staying the same is greater than the pain of change.'*
> **Tony Robbins**

In a business world that is so very different to the one in which I worked and grew up, I often wondered how anyone ever has the time to be productive these days. Since there are so many distractions all vying for your attention these days, the challenge is finding a way to make the best use of your valuable time.

How can you increase your productivity in today's business world? The simple answer is 'I don't know' and this book is not a 'how-to' manual. What I will say is that my work and life experiences over many years have inspired plenty of reflection. At the end of the day, it all depends on where you work, what you do and the type of values and culture that you personally aspire to or the one that is present in your workplace.

I have worked for private businesses, government and not-for-profits as well as owning my own business. This has given me a wide range of experience with different cultures and practices in the workforce. The biggest change that I have experience over this time is the yearning to get 'more for less'. Consumption has changed from the quality of a product to the price of the product, which to me is false economy for us and the planet.

If you are providing goods or a service, how do you sell more of those goods and services? How do you get to more people so that you can sell more of those goods and services? What is business all about really? What is the cost to you and your business? What is your return on the investment of the precious time and energy that is expended by you and your employees? Is it about getting more customers or doing your very best to retain the ones you have? Most importantly, are you providing a good or service that is environmentally friendly and sustainable?

Many years ago, I spoke to a real estate agent who was telling me how difficult it was to keep up with his business. He said that for one query he would have to deal with five points of contact. If he did not answer his phone immediately, then he would have so much more work to do later. I was surprised by what he had said, so I asked him to explain. The agent continued:

> *'If I do not answer the call immediately, then the client will leave a voice message, which results in a text. Then the client will also ring the office to see if I am there. If I am not at the office, the client will leave a message with the receptionist who then sends me an email advising me to ring the client. Sometimes, the client will even send me an email directly. This is all just from one client. Add to that my other clients, as well as the queries from prospective new clients.'*

In a real estate firm, there tend to be real estate agents, a receptionist, property manager, accountant, administrative staff, settlement clerks, technical support team and more. Reflecting back on that real estate agent and his firm, it was no wonder they needed so many staff members. Then there is the regular maintenance and administration that is required to keep company websites updated and emails, Facebook, Instagram, Twitter, WhatsApp, LinkedIn and whatever else is out there now that requires regular monitoring. To top it all off, businesses these days have to be hyper vigilant about cyber security and protecting their data, information, client privacy and business accountability from external and internal threats. These all result in indirect costs to providing goods and services.

When I started work, most administrative and accounting jobs were done manually, using a manual typewriter, a manual calculator, pen, paper and our brains. In fact, I once went for a job interview as an accountant. When I arrived, I was handed two sheets of paper that had rows of figures on each of them, which I was asked to add up using only my brain. When I was finished doing these manual calculations, I handed the sheets back to the interviewer who then asked me to wait. A few moments later, the interviewer returned and immediately asked me when I could start. Bemused and flattered, I asked him if he wanted to see my resume and references, which he declined. I was then told that I was the last applicant that they were interviewing for the job and the first to get all answers correct. Then he asked again, 'When can you start?'

TIME MANAGEMENT

In most of the accounting and legal practices that I worked in, I had to allocate my working time into six-minute units. Even a short phone call was a minimum of six minutes charged to the client. I was required to be productive and charge to clients at least 75 per cent of the time, or six hours out of my eight-hour workday. When I was not working on a client's file, this was usually classified as administrative work, like doing timesheets. This would normally have been relatively easy to do if I was doing the same work all day long, however, as a tax accountant, I was working on many different clients' files each and every day. These files were all at various stages of completion. Every time I took a phone call from a client, read a letter or did any filing related to a particular client, I was meant to look at my watch and make a record of how long each task took and record it manually on a time sheet. I had to record the time I started and finished for anything that related to all the clients I had dealt with on that day. This, to me, was the ultimate clock watching to the point where, now that I am retired, I no longer wear a watch.

Yes, I worked in some very busy accounting practices, however, reflecting back, it was a lot less stressful than dealing with all of the additional social media and other technological challenges businesses face today. Even today, I still find it easier to keep a paper trail just in case the computer crashes or power fails.

An advert by *Inventium* read:

> '*Imagine if you could increase your productivity by more than 20 per cent… Email. Social media. Endless pings and dings. We live in a world littered with digital distraction and temptation. And when we need to do focused and impactful work, protecting that time is precious. Now is the time to reinvent your workday. In just ten minutes per week for 6 weeks,* Inventium's *online WORKDAY REINVENTION PROGRAM will take you through the latest productivity research from psychology and neuroscience and give you evidence-based strategies that will help you transform your work habits, turbo charge your output, and optimise your work hours.*'

When I showed this advert to my friend, he asked if I had written it, which made me laugh. However, I am sure there are many businesses out there today that would gladly sign up immediately.

OLD VS NEW

As I reflect back over more than fifty years of my working life and acknowledge just how much things have changed, I realise that, like all things, some of my experiences have been good, while others, at least from my perspective, have created even more challenges and stress in my everyday working life.

When I commenced work, things were very different. Oh, there were many of the things that we have today—yes, like cars, which in those days were manual and used leaded fuel. If you wanted to pay more, you could even get an automatic. I used to drive a manual car, the red postie wagon as it was called. I now have an automatic car and feel a bit like a robot steering it instead of actually being fully in control of driving.

Laptop computers, tablets and mobile phones were non-existent in my early years and not in any workplace that I worked in until the mid-1980s. In fact, I still remember working in a law firm that still had an operating manual telephone switchboard, where the operator would connect an incoming or outgoing call by inserting a pair of phone plugs into the appropriate jack plug. Above each jack was a light which turned on when the phone was lifted by the receiver. There were plugs and cords going everywhere. One day, I had to relieve the switchboard operator and that day mayhem was created. I even had nightmares that night being caught up in the wires and cutting people off mid conversation.

Most things were still manually operated until the early to mid-1980s like the cash register, typewriter and calculator. My calculator had a paper roll so that you could see the figure you had just typed. This was great as you could immediately check your accuracy as you went along.

I thought it would be good to do a brief comparison between the typewriter and computer.

Productivity Challenges—Punished for Doing Good

THEN: Typewriter	NOW: Computer
Manual—later versions were electronic.	Electronic—with battery backup.
Power—no power source required.	Power—needs a continuous power source.
QWERTY keyboard design is used.	QWERTY keyboard design is used and has an additional numeric section on the right side.
Information is stored on paper, which is not environmentally friendly, especially with the amount of information being produced today. Although I often wonder if we are creating information overload. I prefer to read a 'hard copy'.	Information can be stored digitally, which means no paper. Virtual storage space can be 'unlimited' depending on your provider, USB size or hard drive storage. However, from my experience, if backups are not done regularly, then like the wind, 'poof' and the information is gone.
Correction of errors—before whiteout and spellcheck, correcting errors meant that errors were obvious, or you started again.	Correction of errors—with spellcheck and other computer enhancements, a simple keystroke can correct any errors.
Ink is required to produce a document.	Virtual production and transmission of documents requires power and an internet connection.
Biggest advantage—great for manual operation and producing small documents and you don't need to rely on any external energy.	Biggest advantage—you don't need to know how to spell and you can produce and digitally send volumes of information.

As can be seen in the brief comparison, every system has its advantages and disadvantages. Whilst in this modern era it is so much easier to present, produce and disseminate information, it is also more important than ever to protect and secure your equipment and information.

I am all for growing and learning, however there has been so much change in the way we work now that it is hard to keep up. I have to admit that I feel as though change and adaption is required so rapidly that I feel as though I am being left behind. It is no wonder there is so much stress being reported when there are so many expectations to keep up with the latest mobile phone, software upgrade or other gadget.

BALANCE OR BURNOUT

Most of my work history has been in the field of accounting, although my first job was with the police department doing clerical work. While I am very grateful for that job, I remember getting so bored with what I now refer to as 'paper shuffling'. One of my duties involved looking through files upon files of documents to find the registered owner of a vehicle. Finding the document was easy when they were filed in alphabetical order, however some people had a weird and wonderful understanding of what 'alphabetical' meant. After that job, I worked in many varied roles. It was the variety and differences in the work that I chose that inspired me the most. The job I enjoyed the most was the one that presented the most challenges. However, I see now that when we are faced with too many challenges and there is not enough work-life balance, this can, as it did for me, result in burnout.

When you continue to work, soldiering on and ignoring your physical and mental health, sooner or later your body will let you know. The symptoms can either be subtle or intense. In my case they were intense. After years and years of being a work horse, I developed adrenal fatigue with a number of other symptoms. The most consistent symptom that I was experiencing was persistent tiredness. Finally, my doctor said to me, 'After two years of seeing you and trying to find a cause for your 'tiredness', I realised that you minimise your symptoms.' I would say to my doctor that I was feeling extremely tired, whereas in reality, I was exhausted. Continually driving myself at work, whilst experiencing exhaustion, ultimately resulted in burnout.

The more work I did, the more work I was expected to do. This became a vicious cycle. I lived to work and worked to live which eventually took its toll not only on me but on all my family.

PUNISHED FOR DOING GOOD

Hindsight is a wonderful thing, and whilst I can honestly say that I enjoyed most of the jobs I had, many of them were not very supportive. My superiors in these jobs were very happy for me to work the extra hours. However, not once was I offered any support, nor did they ask why I was working extra time, let alone offer to pay me extra. I also did not stand up for myself. Give me back the time clocks where you clocked in when you started work and clocked out when you left. This recorded all the time you were at work and you were paid accordingly. The people that started at 8:30 am and finished at 5:00 pm were way smarter than I was. Now, I would definitely stay home, if I were sick and would only go back to work when I had completely recovered.

Most centres and businesses are run on a yearly budget. These budgets are usually prepared in April for the following financial year, July to June. Actual expenditure is compared to budgeted figures regularly throughout the year. At the end of March, each centre is able to predict how they will go financially into the next few months. If a centre has spent more than was budgeted in March, then adjustments to spending are made where possible. On the other hand, if a centre has been especially frugal with the expenditure, then in May and June there seemed to be a spending spree. This would not have raised any alarm for me if the money was spent on essential items, however often this was not the case.

As the state business manager for a large not-for-profit, it was my job to support and administer the ongoing operations for the various centres. All of the centres were run so well and seem to survive on the smell of an oily rag, so I could not understand the spending spree. At the end of the financial year, it became blatantly obvious. If a centre had gone over budget, it seemed to be tolerated, with maybe a few questions. However, if the centre had a surplus at the end of the year, the unspent amount would have to be returned. Unless the centre could justify why the full budget had not been spent in that financial year, not only did they have to return the unspent funds, but the same amount was taken off the next financial year. Punished for doing good. No wonder most of the centres went on a spending spree to make sure the entire budget was spent.

Speaking to others about this accounting practice, I was told that this was also how government departments worked. I was horrified. No wonder we hear of so much wasted spending. Unfortunately, I only worked in this organisation for three years which was not enough time to implement any changes. Coming from private practice, I should have suspected something when, as part of my interview for the position, I was told, 'We are a not-for-profit and we can't afford to pay you very much.' My response to this statement was, 'I don't see a not-for-profit organisation any differently than a for-profit organisation. The only difference is where the profits go. The more frugally the organisation functions the more people can be supported.'

Yes, I got the job, however I definitely was not paid enough for its demands. As my aunt said, 'Two-thirds paid, one-third voluntary work.' Still to this day, I cannot understand why government agencies and not-for-profit organisations are not being supported to be more frugal. However, as I look further into what is going on there seems to be a mentality of punishment if you do not fit into the box and comply. Too many regulations and not enough freedoms in order to thrive.

COMMUNICATION—POWER OF WORDS

'Ditch the spin tactics and 'overtly corporate' style of communicating in favour of being more human. Make it easier, quicker, relevant, interactive and fun.'
Gael Adams-Burton

For business professionals, clear and effective communication with clients, customers, colleagues and other professionals is vital to the success of the business. Research has shown that 70 to 90 per cent of our communication is nonverbal whereas only 10 to 30 per cent is verbal. Nonverbal communication like body movement, posture, facial expression, eye contact and hand gestures all contribute to how we communicate and understand each other. In verbal communication, tone of voice can matter as much as or even more than the substance of what you are saying. Business is often conducted by text, email or other forms of communication where the nonverbal cues get lost. My preferred way of communicating is face-to-face. Some research indicates that in modern times verbal communication is only 7 per cent which seems more realistic now as most of the communication today is done by email, text, social media and rarely posted mail.

It often takes much more time to send an email or a text than it does to just pick up the phone and get an immediate response to a query. Sometimes the action that was requested via an email is not very clear so the constant back and forth can get extremely frustrating. What is written in an email can be misleading, which can lead to confusion and misunderstanding. Misunderstandings are more easily rectified verbally, meaning that if the quality of the communication has been lost in translation, it can result in ongoing written and even legal disputes which are definitely not good for business and can become very costly.

Anyone who has ever played a game called Chinese whispers or telephone as a child, will know what I mean. This game starts off with a group of people sitting in a circle. One person whispers a message to the person next to them, who then whispers what they heard to the next person, and so on, until they have reached the last person. Each recipient has just a single opportunity to hear the message before passing on exactly what they heard. The last person repeats out loud what they heard. Writing down the original message and comparing it with the final message often produces some very interesting and funny results. Whilst this was a game I played and enjoyed as a child, it would also be a great game for adults as it is essentially about the quality of communication, both sent and received.

What and how we communicate can have a huge impact on how the recipients of that communication feel. Sometimes it is not the words that are said but the meaning that is portrayed behind the words. This has recently been highlighted in the media when certain ministers reflected on their feelings, thoughts and understanding of the impact of sexual harassment in the workplace. Sometimes, it is not about the words themselves, but how someone feels during and after a conversation. It is great to get people inspired by the message that is being portrayed however it is also important for the message to have integrity.

Are your beliefs and values congruent with and evident in the words and actions that are being shown, or do you let the thoughts of others affect the way you approach the world?

> *'It is never about the announcements, the number of clicks, or even how much engagement you achieve, it's about driving business results.'*
> **Andrea Greenhous**

When I read the statement above, relating to marketing and communication, it stirred an emotional response in me and I made a judgement regarding the integrity of the message. It is important for a business to have a good workplace culture, strong values and respectful communication in all aspects of business and life.

INTIMATE COMMUNICATION

The way people communicate with work colleagues, acquaintances and friends is often different to the way things are communicated within families and intimate relationships.

When I was young, my mother said to me, 'If you can't say anything nice then don't say anything at all.' However, not everybody got that message. Whilst I still agree with what my mother said, for me on reflection, I did not let people know when I was hurt or angered by what they said or did. I always had to be the 'good girl' and not express my anger, or I would get a clip over the ear. As an adult, I soon learnt that keeping anger bottled up inside was not helpful for my wellbeing.

I have since learnt that our thoughts create our reality, so the quality of our thoughts create the quality of our reality. By continually bottling up my feelings, I noticed that, like a volcano, eventually there would be an eruption—sometimes over the smallest of things, which was totally inappropriate. However, as with most things in life, this is simply another learning opportunity. I noticed that the difference between an open and honest discussion and an argument was the emotional reaction that I experienced. I needed to recognise and acknowledge when I was having an emotional reaction and take personal responsibility for my response. It is not appropriate to inflict our emotions and feelings onto others. We are energetic beings and we need to feel our emotions in order to heal.

Whilst I strongly believe that we all need to take responsibility for our own emotional reactions, this does not mean that we should allow ourselves to be walked over either. Recently, I have heard some amazing conversation and discussion on sexual harassment and sexualised behaviours and what informs 'consent'. Such open and honest discussions which, were previously never discussed in public and sometimes not even behind closed doors, are now in the spotlight. Interpreting whether you have consent is very complicated and definitely not clear. 'Yes' does not always mean 'yes', just as 'no' does not always mean 'no'.

Consent is when one person agrees or gives permission to another person to do something. To give consent, you need to be fully informed of what you are giving your consent to. It means agreeing to an action based on your knowledge of what that action involves, its possible consequences and always having the option of saying no. The term consent is used in many areas such as law, medicine, research and sexual relationships. Consent means freely choosing to say 'yes' to a sexual activity, a choice that must be made without coercion, pressure, guilt or threats. Saying 'yes' to one thing doesn't mean 'yes' to everything.

Workplace relationships are very different to personal relationships and often the boundaries become blurred. Clear, honest and respectful communication make all relationships better especially intimate and sexual relationships. Asking for and obtaining consent shows respect for yourself and the other person. It eliminates the entitlement that one person might feel over the other. The power over or presumptions of entitlement within a workplace is currently under scrutiny. Neither your body nor your sexuality belong to anyone else.

The sad reality is that no longer can you presume anything. Being taken out to dinner or for a drink may seem wonderful and sweet, as long as there are no conditions attached, whether explicit or implicit. There is often a presumption that if someone gives you something then there is an expectation of something in return. In other words, is it safe to receive? Are all gifts conditional? If so, then every so-called conditional gift should clearly state what the expectation is if the gift is accepted. Does the act of giving or receiving come with energetic attachments? Recently, a male friend asked me what a 'sleazebag' meant. Personally, I found this very hard to describe in words, however when I asked my female friends if they knew what a 'sleaze' was, there was no resistance or doubt. Most times, the woman would describe it as someone who made them feel 'icky' and horrible.

At this profound time in history, there is a global resonance from women who are saying 'enough'. Enough with all the bullshit and incongruence between what is verbally spoken and the energetic intent. I am sure that there are also many wonderful men who would say 'enough is enough'. For those to whom this incongruence applies: Do not take away our innocence with your manipulative and coercive behaviour.

USE AND ABUSE OF POWER

Words are powerful and they can either lift you up or bring you down. Music and sound can be just as powerful. Recently, I have been challenged by what meaning is trying to be portrayed by the words that have been spoken. Words without corresponding actions are meaningless. The meaning of the words 'I love you' is very confusing for someone who has experienced family abuse of any kind, as are any other words that do not match up with the utterer's behaviour.

Whether in the workplace or home, many behaviours are similar in either arena. If you need your job for financial reasons and you fear speaking up in case it upsets someone then that is not a safe workplace. Constantly hiding your true self for fear of losing your job or being rejected by your colleagues can be restrictive. Feeling like you are walking on eggshells, not knowing if it is safe to express your authentic self, is debilitating. The irony is that things that have been going on behind closed doors for a very long time are now being identified in the workplace. What has always been ironic to me is knowing that someone can act very aggressively at home and yet in a similar situation in the workplace they can be very respectful.

Behaviours can change if there is a choice and willingness to do so. If you want to make a positive impact on the world, be conscious of how you are expressing yourself energetically, through words and actions. What I have learnt is that you never really know how a person is left feeling after your interaction with them. A person may not remember what you actually said to them, however they will remember how you made them feel.

> *'A healthy relationship doesn't drag you down.
> It inspires you to be better.'*
> **Mandy Hale**

2

Policy and Procedures vs Trust

POLICIES AND PROCEDURES

Every workplace is different. Its size will usually dictate the type of induction you receive when you start working there. From my work experience, I went from a half-hour tour of the office layout and staff introductions to a whole two-week of induction which included reading three large files of office policy and procedure manuals and various information classes before actually starting work.

The intention of workplace policy and procedures manual is to guide the new employee to various aspects of the business, outlining clear expectations and providing a consistent approach to managing workplace issues. Policies are intended to communicate the connection between the organisation's vision and values and its day-to-day operations, whereas procedures are intended to explain a specific action plan to carry out the intention of the policy.

According to WorkPlace Plus, the six must-have policies for your workplace are:

1. Workplace health and safety (WHS) policy, highlighting any potential workplace risks or hazards;
2. Anti-discrimination policy, promoting equal employment opportunity;
3. Privacy policy, regarding the disclosure of an employee's personal details;
4. Leave policy, outlining the guidelines and requirements for accessing leave entitlements;
5. Complaints and grievances policy, with options for conflict resolution and employee assistance;
6. Performance management policy, outlining the process for performance.

The above-mentioned policies are an umbrella for several other essential policies, including:

- Appropriate workplace conduct or code of conduct, discussing respect and responsibility;
- Building evacuation policy, including your safety procedure for an emergency evacuation;
- Bullying and harassment policy, including sexual harassment;
- Mentally healthy workplace policy, promoting employee wellbeing and providing support;
- Pandemic policy, preventing and responding to an outbreak, including infection control.

Anti-discrimination:

- Disability access and inclusion policy, promoting equal opportunity for people with disabilities;
- Diversity policy, promoting gender parity and cultural diversity.

Policies such as the appropriate use of IT and social media at work and domestic/family violence could fall under both workplace health and safety and anti-discrimination policies. Some workplaces may also choose to include policies around lgbt inclusion, vaccination, working from home, sustainability, smoking, alcohol and drugs and/or use of company property. As the workplace culture evolves and community values change, the HR polices should also follow suit.

In today's world, we have more and more workplace policies and procedures, yet there seems to be less and less workplace satisfaction. Why is this? Were you given the office manual to read when you started your job? How big was it, did you read it all and was it relevant to your working environment? More importantly, did you fully understand all that you have read in your workplace manual?

At the end of the day, it is all well and good having wonderful policies and procedures that say the right things, but unless they are modelled and implemented in the workplace, they are functionally useless. Whilst policies and procedures are part of the operating business practice, they are not legal contracts. By contrast, a privacy policy and terms and conditions are two different types of legal documents which have the purpose of protecting your business from liability and legal claims.

PRIVACY POLICY AND TERMS AND CONDITIONS

When you are starting any business, you need to take steps to successfully get your business off the ground and set it on a path that will bring you success and help you meet the needs of your customers. Starting a business can be simple, however it is important to do some research on any legal requirements.

Once you decide on what you want to do, it might be helpful to select a name for your business. Often, checking the registry of business names will verify if someone else is already using that name; if not, then you may wish to register your business name. Choosing a business structure such as a sole trader, partnership or company will often depend on the life stage of your business. Applying for your Australian Business Number (ABN), setting up a bank account, selecting an accounting and record keeping system, enquiring about any insurances and registering for Goods and Services Tax (GST) are some of other matters to look into.

If you decide to set up a business website or mobile app, one of the most important parts of launching is creating the terms and conditions and privacy policy agreements for your particular business. These are legal agreements that are incredibly valuable for both you and your customers, because not only do they inform people about everything that they are agreeing to when they start using your services, but they also protect your company against legal claims.

As a customer, before purchasing or engaging with any business or service online, you are required to tick the box which says that you have read and understood the terms and conditions and/or privacy policy relating to that transaction. Do you ever read the terms and conditions and privacy statement? Do you understand them? Do you tick the box anyway, regardless of whether you have read and understood what they say? I admit that I have ticked the box even though I have rarely fully understood what I have read.

I consider myself relatively intelligent, with a university degree as well as having worked in a law firm, yet even so, I still don't understand all of what is written in most of the terms and conditions and privacy policies that I am ticking the box for. There is so much legal jargon that I wonder if anyone, other than the lawyers that wrote them, ever really understands what they were agreeing too. What I have found, at times, is that one paragraph in the terms and conditions seems to be contradicted by another paragraph. In other words, what do they really mean? The problem is that if you want that product then you have to tick the box to proceed—you don't really have the option to say no. Consequently, most of these agreements are ticked with a great degree of trust. With the internet and social media, privacy and related policies may have been created with good intent initially but are likely now defunct.

TRUST

Trust is a precious commodity both in business and in our personal relationships.

The sad thing is that over the years our trust has been eroded. I remember my father telling me that he got his first loan for money to buy our first home with only a handshake. Throughout history a handshake, which dates back to the fifth century B.C. in Ancient Greece, was a symbol of peace, signalling friendship, and was used in finalising a business agreement and/or transaction. This way of doing business conferred trust from one person to another. However, even before social distancing disrupted this age-old habit of a handshake, the trust people had in business, politics and each other had been well and truly eroded.

The most important business and brand asset is trust, especially in their relationships with customers, clients, employees and other stakeholders. Every interaction a business engages in is an opportunity to nurture relationships and build trust. There was once a time when executives knew the importance of their companies' reputation and they were prepared to protect that reputation at all costs. Firms with strong positive reputations attract better people. These businesses are perceived as providing more value, which often allowed them to charge a premium for their product or service. Their customers are loyal and often buy a broader range of products and services from them. The reputation and trust of people and businesses are both very highly valued.

Whatever happened to trust when only 22 per cent of people globally trust business leaders and 32 per cent distrust business leaders? This leaves the other half of the population undecided—a pretty sad indictment on modern society.

In an article dated 18 September 2019, an Ipsos (Market Research Company) poll revealed that scientists are considered the most trustworthy profession in the world, followed closely by doctors. Of the global public, six in ten rated scientists as trustworthy and just one in ten considered them untrustworthy. The next most trustworthy profession according to the study is teachers, whereas politicians were ranked as the least trusted group globally. I wonder how much these statistics have changed over the last two years.

Somebody said to me recently, 'People, businesses or government authorities, would not do anything, allow anything to happen or produce anything that is 'harmful' to us. When this was said to me, quite innocently, I felt like screaming, 'ARE YOU KIDDING?' My jaw dropped and I was speechless, something that rarely happens to me. This was 'blind trust'.

What immediately comes to mind is thalidomide, a drug which was reported to cause the deaths and deformities of babies in the 1960s and yet it is FDA-approved and still in use today. Then there is asbestos, which is a naturally occurring mineral with soft, flexible fibres that are heat-resistant. Exposure to asbestos causes cancers, progressive lung diseases, mesothelioma and asbestosis. Asbestos may still be used in hundreds of US consumer products. Add to that the dangerous chemicals that have been used, like formaldehyde, mercury, lead, hazardous and toxic air pollutants, glyphosate (pesticide chemical), PFAS (polyfluoroalkyl substances), PCBs (polychlorinated biphenyls) and cigarettes.

Recently, I have been challenged with messages espoused by governments and medical authorities. As a result of previously having adverse reactions to safe procedures and medications, I can no longer trust what is promoted as 'safe'. Research into alternatives has created even more confusion. I need to take responsibility for what is best for my health and wellbeing. Previous experiences have proven that what may be safe for others is not safe for me. Now, I have learnt to rely on my instincts or if unsure I use muscle testing or kinesiology as biofeedback to confirm what is in the interests of my highest good. Blind trust in our regulatory authorities is not being responsible.

Author Stephen R Covey in *The Speed of Trust* and *Smart Trust: Creating Prosperity, Energy and Joy in a Low Trust World* explained how the profits of businesses would actually increase if businesses trusted their employees and clients. These books would be well worth reading for any business that wanted to reduce costs and increase profits. You can trust too much and get burnt, or not trust enough and miss out on opportunities that inspire and engage others. Using 'smart trust' balances the extremities between not enough or too much trust.

For a short moment, reflect on who you trust or someone who first placed their trust in you. Who comes to mind when you think about the people, businesses, companies, charities, doctors, religious institutions, police, governments (all levels), service providers or their representatives, family members or anyone else you have interacted with throughout your life? More importantly, how good did it feel when you were given the opportunity to show that you could be trusted?

I have had a great deal of trust given to me during my lifetime both in business and my personal life. In one job I was given carte blanche when it came to managing the business and personal affairs for my boss. His business had over $3 million per year in turnover with me being sole signatory to the cheque and bank accounts. I had full access and passwords to all his finances, and I probably should have framed the reference that I was given. Even in my private life, I was asked by a friend to look after their house and business while they were overseas for an extended period of time. As she said, 'You get the house, cars, business and bank accounts and I get the husband and the kids.' One friend even said that I was too honest.

Later in life, I was challenged by trust issues in a personal capacity. As I reflected on who I personally trusted, this was much harder to identify. Whilst many people trusted me, I was deceived by others. It got to the point where I could no longer trust myself or the decisions that I was making. I was too trusting of others and they let me down. There were times when I sold my soul for money and did things that were out of integrity with my values and beliefs. This was hard to admit. However, I am sure that I am not the only one who has ever done this.

Building trust, in the long term, can be way more profitable and more beneficial to all.

Just imagine how much you would save in a business if:

- You could trust your employees to do what is needed to fully support you and your business;
- Your clients were proud and appreciative of the work that is done and gladly pay you for your services;
- You did not need a human resource department or a policy and procedures manual, just a one-page list of values to work by;
- You didn't need a debt collection department or lawyers to deal with any litigation, because all your customers were gladly paying you on completion of the job; and
- Finally, you did not need to have an IT department that had to consistently monitor the system for corruption errors, hackers or breakdowns.

Sure, I get it, I can hear you saying, live in the real world. Well, maybe that is something worth creating and we can start by restoring trust in ourselves and others.

In the past trust was valued so much more than it is today. People would often finalise business transactions on a handshake. Their word was their bond. In other words, you could trust what they said and they would do what they said they were going to do. On top of that, there was a care factor and a sense of pride with all the work that they did and employees would be valued and fairly paid. You could rely on the fact that the work would be done properly and you would be charged a fair price. As the saying goes, 'A fair day's work for a fair day's pay.'

3

Local vs Global— Sustainability

LOCAL vs GLOBAL

> *'Economic localisation is the key to sustaining biological and cultural diversity—to sustaining life itself. The sooner we shift towards the local, the sooner we will begin healing our planet, our communities and ourselves.'*
> **Helena Norberg-Hodge**

In the last few years, the important reality of local versus global has never been more evident. What has been eye-opening, and a real awakening, is just how reliant our country is on people, produce and products from other countries. Whilst globalisation can be great, the ramifications when businesses were shut down have been very obvious. As well, it has really highlighted just how much of a global economy this world has become. No matter what country you are living in, there will be a reliance on another country for something. Trades between countries involve more than just borrowing a cup of sugar from your neighbour.

What is traded will depend on the requirement of the specific country and whether that country is developed or developing, rich or poor, relies on education or tourism, or trades manufactured goods, agricultural or mined resources. There is a belief that manufacturing is mainly in developing countries as these countries can usually provide a cheaper workforce. Is that belief really true, or is it all about the ever-increasing profit expectations of the larger companies?

In a recent newsletter, local politician Libby Coker, speaking about economic growth, stated:

> *'Expending our advanced manufacturing base which has slumped from 30 per cent of GDP (Gross Domestic Product) in the 60s to just under 6 per cent last year. The Centre for Future Work has recently estimated that of the 36 developed OECD (Organisation for Economic Co-operation and Development) countries, Australia ranks last in self-sufficiency in manufactured goods with Australia only producing two thirds of the manufacturing goods it consumes compared to Germany at 118 per cent and Sweden at 112 per cent for example. Other rich, high wage countries do manufacturing very well. We should too and COVID-19 gives us that opportunity.'*

Besides global trade, there is also global travel. For many years, people have travelled all over the world. Since the Australian borders have been shut to the rest of the world due to the pandemic, travel has also been limited to destinations closer to home. Ordinarily, people would travel either for business or pleasure. Now, because many flights have been grounded and travel restricted, the plight of many Australian residents who have been stuck overseas has been highlighted because they have been unable to return home. Freedoms have been greatly restricted in so many ways worldwide.

HOME

With the ability and freedom to travel and work anywhere in the world, people are making many different choices about where they call home. There is a song by Paul Young called *Wherever I Lay My Hat That's My Home*.

Planet Earth is not the dustbin of the universe; it is our home. When we start looking at Earth as our home, would we then consider doing some things very differently? Your whole perspective changes when you are challenged to look at things differently. For example, is the roof over your head your house or your home. Depending on how you define that roof over your head, this will impact the way you value what you have. A house is just a structure, but when you feel attached to that structure, it becomes a home. Home is where your heart is. A home is any place where you feel comfortable enough to be yourself. It does not matter whether your home is outside in nature or in an apartment, as long as your heart is there, then this is your home. Being in lock down allowed people to focus on how they feel within their houses or homes. On top of that, many people had to re-evaluate how comfortable and affordable their homes really were.

The following poem titled *And the People Stayed Home* by Catherine (Kitty) O'Meara of Madison, Wisconsin, penned in March 2020, explains the lives of many people all over the world during this time:

And people stayed home
and read books and listened
and rested and exercised
and made art and played
and learned new ways of being
and stopped
and listened deeper
someone meditated
someone prayed
someone danced
someone met their shadow
and people began to think differently
and people healed
and in the absence of people who lived in ignorant ways,
dangerous, meaningless and heartless,
even the earth began to heal
and when the danger ended
and people found each other
grieved for the dead people
and they made new choices
and dreamed of new visions
and created new ways of life
and healed the earth completely
just as they were healed themselves.

A house is made of walls and beams and a home is filled with love and dreams.

SUSTAINABILITY

'We are not going to get out of this environmental mess by science and policy alone.'
Vance Martin

'The destiny of humans cannot be separated from the destiny of earth. We are in trouble now because we do not have a good story.'
Thomas Berry

> it's 3:23 in the morning
> and I'm awake
> because my great great grandchildren
> won't let me sleep
> my great great grandchildren
> ask me in dreams
> what did you do while the planet was plundered?
> what did you do when the earth was unraveling?
>
> surely you did something
> when the seasons started failing?
>
> as the mammals, reptiles, birds were all dying?
>
> did you fill the streets with protest
> when democracy was stolen?
>
> what did you do
> once
> you
> knew?

Many years ago, I heard the poem *Hieroglyphic Stairway* by Drew Dellinger. The words 'what did you do once you knew?' have never left me and have driven me ever since.

There is a great deal more to this poem, however the line 'what did you do when you knew' created my blessed unrest. What have I done and what will I do? What actions can we all take to help change our highly consumptive culture? Well, I can start today by critically looking at what I personally do every day and re-evaluate my needs as distinct from my wants.

Through education and awareness, we have the ability to reflect on how we are personally contributing to the pollution of our planet. When you throw your rubbish away, where is away? Rubbish never actually goes away; it just becomes a problem for someone else. If you are living in suburbia there is a weekly rubbish collection, so it is out of sight, out of mind. Yes, we now have recycling however we are creating more rubbish than can be recycled. Our current rubbish tips are overflowing and when our country can no longer send the rubbish overseas then, all of a sudden, we are forced to find a different solution. Years ago, I found out that I had purchased a house that was built over a tip, which explained the cracks in the house due to the movement of the ground. For all you know, you could be living on top of a rubbish dump.

Currently, I am blessed to be living in a beautiful part of the world where there seems to be very little obvious pollution, and often until it is right in your face, it is as though it doesn't exist. In 2019, Australia suffered massive bushfires, and the smoke from those fires impacted communities far and wide. This time, the pollution was in our face and could not be ignored. These fires created so much physical and environmental destruction, as well as having an ongoing impact on our physical health, emotional wellbeing and other needs.

Then along came the COVID-19 virus, impacting an already vulnerable population. There was a massive awareness campaign with ever changing rules and regulations that was relentless. It seemed as though everyone was now more conscious of their own health, personal hygiene and their impact on the health and wellbeing of themselves and others. This proved just how quickly people were able to adapt and change. Most of us tend to focus on 'not getting sick', rather than on improving our immune system to stay healthier overall. Our mitochondria, the tiny energy factories within our body's cells, are the key to optimal health and healing. Mitochondria generate the energy that we need to stay alive and well, however with today's lifestyle it is hard to escape mitochondrial damage.

This particular time felt as if we were all actors in a global movie which had a deep and sinister fearful plot and the only way that we would survive is to comply and concede with all of the requests. It felt as if the responsibility for our own health and wellbeing would be taken out of our hands because there was another solution. At the time of the global pandemic, it was made abundantly clear how much we had to rely on others for our own protection. We were given extra financial support to make sure that our basic needs for food, water, housing and safety were covered. Sadly, for some people during this time, their top priority was toilet paper. This period in history made me really evaluate what was important to me and how important it was for me to take personal responsibility for my own wellbeing. Just for a short moment, stop and think about what has become much more important for you during this time.

What happened to 'love and connection' during this time? A study completed many years ago with babies in an orphanage proved that babies could survive without love and connection, however they really thrived when both were present.

The sustainability of our planet depends on the actions of its people. The actions of the people will depend on how they perceive their personal sustainability. In order to change the trajectory, we must become more conscious of what we really value and what we are prepared to do differently to leave a healthier planet for our future generations. People have proven that they can change quickly if required to.

From an old Native American prophecy:

> *When the Earth is ravaged and the animals are dying,*
> *a new tribe of people shall come onto the Earth*
> *from many colours, classes, creeds*
> *and who by their actions and deeds*
> *shall make the Earth green again.*

INEQUITABLE PRACTICES

Years ago, I had the opportunity to travel to Kenya on an inspirational journey, during which I learnt so much about myself and my travel companions. During my time there I stayed in five-star accommodation, experienced a five-day safari in the Serengeti seeing a wide variety of wild animals up close and personal, visited three Maasai villages and a village for people with different abilities. I had an in-depth conversation with Dr Jack Githae, a traditional African herbal practitioner, healer and proponent of alternative medicine. Then I was invited to visit orphanages and the local slums which showed a different lifestyle. Many of the people I met had so little and yet seemed so happy. I also learnt about the invisible prisons that can be created by the value of the currency. As of writing in April 2021, one Australian dollar converts to 82.45 Kenyan shillings. Currently, the average price of a one- to three-bedroom house in Kenya is 14.4 million Kenyan shillings which converts to 174,651.30 Australian dollars. Is it any wonder that the Kenyan people think we are so rich to be able to afford to travel?

Now, let's have a look at what I see as real inequity in Australia. While every single human being has 24 hours in every day, we are definitely not equal in how we are paid.

The CEO of IPD Education, Andrew Barkla, is the highest-paid chief executive in Australia, earning an eye-watering $38 million per year which amounts to $104,109 a day or $13,013 per hour for an eight-hour day. IDP Education is a company which offers international students placements in Australia as well as English language tests. In 2020, the average annual salary in Australia was $85,982 therefore 442 people can be employed for the same yearly salary as Andrew Barkla. For students, the current Austudy allowance is approximately $541.70 per fortnight, which is $14,084 per year. Therefore, what this CEO earns per hour, our students earn per year.

According to the Australian Department of Education, Skills and Employment, international education and employment was worth $37.5 billion dollars to the Australian economy for 2019-20. Obviously, the education industry is a very lucrative business. No wonder they want to make sure that the Australian borders remain open to international students. I wonder if Mr Barkla would consider sponsoring a few students.

As at 1 July 2020, the basic minimum wage in Australia is $753.80 per week or annually $39,197.80. So, when I hear that a CEO is paid 38 million or a company director $600,000, this is so unfair, unjust and inequitable. When I found out that the CEO of IPD Education was paid more per year than the Prime Minister of Australia I was horrified. The Prime Minister of Australia should definitely be paid more per year than a company director or CEO of IPD Education.

DECEPTIVE PRACTICES

Hiding behind the fantasy of the greater good only enables avoidance. What should shock everybody reading this book is the assumption that a lot of people believe that the products we buy are safe. The belief that the chemicals like fluoride and chlorine in the water are safe. Here is the problem with those beliefs: there are over 80,000 chemicals in goods and services and very few have been tested for health and safety. Therefore, the precautionary principles are not followed. If it is found out that a specific chemical is harmful it is often taken out and replaced by another chemical that is just as harmful. This is the game that has been played for a very long time.

BPA (bis-phenol A) is a hormone-disrupting chemical used in some plastics, so if you see a label that says 'BPA free', you would assume that BPA must be bad. The reality is that BPA got a bad rap and manufacturers seized on this and labelled certain plastic items 'BPA free' as a selling point. Whilst they took out BPA, they replaced it with its chemical cousin BPS (bis-phenol S). However, the toxicological profiles for BPA and BPS look exactly the same, so the replacement is no better. We have seen this with pesticides, nail polish, e-cigarettes, non-stick fry pans and more. Look up 'forever chemicals' online and you will see many examples. There is no safe replacement of one chemical for another. Smart people see things for how they really are, whereas others see things for how they want them to be.

CHANGING THE ENVIRONMENT

> *'If you give a man a fish, you feed him for a day. If you teach him how to fish, you feed him for life.'*
> **Anonymous**

Prevention is the key to helping people adjust to an ever-deteriorating environment. The challenge is finding what you personally need to support you and your family. From my experience, I have learnt that there is never just one solution, product or remedy that can help everybody. Everything that we do has a flow-on effect and we never know what the unintended consequences will be.

Thomas Edison said in 1890:

> 'The doctor of the future will give no medicine but will interest his patient in the care of the human frame, in diet, and in the cause and prevention of disease.'

Recent events in Australia and across the globe have highlighted how different the solutions to today's disease are. What it has shown is just how rapidly people can change when they feel as though their life is threatened. This is also a good sign to show that if we choose, we can also rapidly change how we impact our environment and Planet Earth, the home we live on. We can avert the environmental crisis if we, as a species, can just as rapidly adapt to Mother Nature's pathway. Viruses in a thriving environment are good for us and they are not the Grim Reaper that we have been encouraged to believe. The beauty of where we are today is that more and more people are challenging these beliefs.

In the video called *TRUTH*, featuring Robert F Kennedy Jr and Dr Zach Bush posted on 13 January 2021, Robert Kennedy Jnr said:

> 'If we had a healthy ecosystem inside and outside (relating to our bodies), polio, HIV (human immunodeficiency virus), TB (tuberculosis) and all other (diseases) that have these environmental connections, would not exist.'

Also in the video, when Dr Zach Bush was asked about the current virus, COVID-19, he said:

> 'What we need to realise is that we are dying from hypoxic injury (meaning partial lack of oxygen), not from some viral infection.'

Dr Zach Bush adds that, 'Sixty-four herbicide and pesticide residues were found in a single glass of Californian wine… we have to stop chemicals in our food systems and we have to do it extremely quickly.'

Dr Bush goes on to say, '*Earth Justice sued the US government months before the pandemic, after seeing that the cyanide levels in our air was higher in our inner-city environment than we had ever measured it before. They sued the government for not putting out warnings for cyanide poisoning. Cyanide poisoning is going to look exactly like COVID-19. We are dying from the poisoning of our own environment. Cyanide is the most common toxin in the air.*'

Medicines are to be found within nature and in our soil systems, which indigenous tribes have always known, so let us co-create with nature and see how quickly we can heal ourselves and our planet. However, firstly we need to notice the toxicity that is created when we resist the reality of the changes that need to be made.

4

People vs Profits—Values

PUBLIC VS PRIVATE

Over the decades, it has become more and more apparent that money carries more value than people both in the workforce and in life. However, there would be no money without people. I often wonder if slavery has really been abolished or if the practice has just been renamed. Even in this time of such dramatic change, with high unemployment rates, the response from many workers is that they love the money but not the job. It also seems rare to find people who value what they are doing more than the money they are receiving. Whilst it is rare to find a workplace that values people above profits, everyone and everything seems to have been reduced to a commodity.

Even our public servants no longer seem to enjoy serving the public. What has been highlighted in the media lately is that many people working in all levels of government seem to be taking their positions as a right, and at times even abuse the privilege of their position. Working conditions, social status and pay for public servants are very different to those working in the private sector. Pay increases for most people in private industries have not happened for many years, and yet public servants get the incremental yearly pay level increase. After doing some research I found that for people with comparable skills and experience, public servants receive total compensation packages that are 25 to 46 per cent higher than private sector employees.

The IZA Institute of Labour Economics (initiated by Deutsche Post Foundation) in collaboration with Flinders University and NILS published a paper in 2017 called 'Public-Private Sector Wage Differentials in Australia.' This paper showed that on average public sector employees earn 5.1 per cent more per hour than the private sector employees. Combining education with gender, this paper also showed that, at the lower end of wage distribution, males with post school qualifications attracted a higher public sector premium than their female counterparts. In contrast, at the higher end of the wage distribution, it is females with post school qualifications who attract the higher wage premium. The paper thus paints a very interesting picture where post-school education appears to favour males in lower-paying public sector jobs and females in higher-paying public sector jobs.

It is well known that the public sector can offer greater job security than the private sector. The public sector has the stability of government finance department behind it, whereas the private sector is more susceptible to closures and redundancies when finances become strained. This was really highlighted in the recent world crisis where only businesses that were classified as 'essential services' were allowed to remain open and other 'non-essential' services and businesses were required to close their doors. The beauty and blessing of entrepreneurs is that they are resilient and are always looking for other options to renew and recover. It is the kind of resilience that nature shows us so often, as witnessed months after the disaster of the bush fires. People are also very resilient, although this is being tested during these trying times. Both the public and private sectors have a role to play. For general businesses without externalities, the private sector is likely to be more efficient and better at job creation. Pollution can be defined as a negative externality. An externality is a cost or benefit that is imposed on a third party who did not agree to incur that cost or benefit. However, the private sector also needs a good public sector to provide, education, healthcare and infrastructure investment.

The private sector consisting mainly of small to medium businesses is the backbone of the Australian economy, creating around 7 million jobs and contributing to 57 per cent of Australia's GDP (gross domestic product) which cements our reputation as a nation of entrepreneurs. Being a business owner can be extremely rewarding and requires the courage to take a risk. Success in business brings with it many advantages as well as disadvantages. As a business owner, you are your own boss, with lifestyle choices and with the modern-day technology more mobility. When you do what you love and love what you do, the money will follow. People often start businesses to be able to have more flexibility with their time and duties, and end up with more stress, more financial risks and more hours working in and on the job. Most people don't even take the chance of starting a business and remain in their jobs (**J**ust **O**ver **B**roke). Yes, I have been employed and owned an accounting practice, bakery and investment properties, so I understand a lot of the benefits and pitfalls.

According to statistics, 20 per cent of start-up businesses fail in their first year and around 60 per cent will go bust within their first three years. In recent years many of the Australian start-up businesses raised financing from alternative financing such as crowdfunding and crowd-investing rather than the traditional lenders. Whilst I am unfamiliar with this source of financing, I suspect it is similar to the old form of cooperatives. The Australian Bureau of Statistics (ABS) defines a small business as someone who employees less than 20 people and a medium sized business employing between 20 to 199 people. Small to medium sized enterprises (SMEs) have different levels of turnover. In 2018/19 financial year 93 per cent of all Australian SMEs had revenue of less than $2 million, 25 per cent had revenue of less than $500,000 and 74.5 per cent had revenue of less than $200,000. Often, the rules that may work very well for big business are detrimental for the small to medium-sized businesses.

PEOPLE VS PROFITS

> *'The universe is composed of subjects to be communed with, not objects to be exploited. Everything has its own voice. Thunder and lightning and stars and planets, flowers, birds, animals, trees—all these have voices, and they constitute a community of existence that is profoundly related.'*
> **Thomas Berry**

I have always believed that people are the most valuable asset that a business has, and therefore people should be valued above profit. If people enjoy their job and have job satisfaction as a consequence, the natural flow should create more profit.

Throughout the global crisis, the Australian State and Federal Government seem to have put human health at the forefront of all decision-making. I have to wonder what is going on, when 'gain of function' research is being allowed to be carried out in one country, while being supported by other countries. Somehow, that super bug that has been created then escapes into the community, creating worldwide 'germ warfare'. Isn't that like closing the gate after the horse has bolted? Stop the practice of creating a 'super bug' in the first place, then we would not have to create something to prevent it from causing harm. If you deal with the cause of the problem, then you don't have to try to find a solution to fix the impact.

Only time will tell what the long-term ramifications of what has been created will be. With borders being closed and communities put into lockdown, people were asked to stay at home, while schools businesses, other than those classified as 'essential services,' were also required to close, prompting a rush on toilet paper.

Sometimes the most basic things can make the most profound changes in your life such as:

- Showing respect and love for yourself and others;
- Realising change is an inevitable part of life;
- Being content, happy and thankful with where you are in life;
- Focusing on what you want in your life, as what you focus on grows;
- Realising that what others think of you is none of your business;
- When you feel good about yourself then you are less likely to take what is said to you personally;
- Learning to hold your tongue and listen to what is being said, before responding. Bringing peace into your words, not anger, noting that the difference between a discussion and an argument is an emotional reaction;
- If you assume that you know something, it can make an 'ass' out of 'u' and 'me';
- Always do your very best in any given moment. If you are feeling emotional, stop and acknowledge your feelings.

During the pandemic, emotions and opinions have been heightened. Usually, I would embrace open and honest discussion however now I have included discussing my opinion about what I am or am not doing with regard to the current situation, as a no-go subject together with politics and religion.

My immune system is already compromised and the last thing I want is to make things worse for myself or others. I am so grateful that in the forefront of all decisions seem to be health, hygiene and saving lives. I grew up in an era where no matter how sick you were, you still went to work—soldiering on regardless. Now, I would no longer do that. What has been highlighted, especially for those working in aged care centres, is if you are sick then stay at home. The irony is that sometimes things are not black and white.

I have breathing difficulties and wearing a mask made things even worse for me hence my doctor provided me with a medical exemption. During times when mandatory mask wearing was required, I hardly left home. In fact, for over 18 months, I have only been out in public to do what has been essential. I know that I am not alone in what I have experienced and that many decisions have had many unintended consequences.

UNSPOKEN MESSAGE

'People don't fake depression… they fake being okay. Remember that. Be kind.'
Robin Williams

Sometimes we do not know what people are going through or why they do what they do. If you can outwardly see frailty or a physical disability this seems to be much more acceptable however many illnesses are not observable.

One day, I had to have a blood test done and when my turn arrived, I approached the nurse. She was taken aback, with a scared and stunned look on her face, and said, 'Where is your mask?' Surprised by the question, I told her I had a medical exemption for not wearing a mask, which I showed her. Then the nurse asked if I had used the hand sanitiser. 'Yes,' I responded. She enquired as to whether I was sick, had a temperature, or had the virus. 'No,' I responded to all of her questions. Then we proceeded to the consulting room where she took my blood.

It is my responsibility to take care of my own health and wellbeing. My doctor wanted to have my vitamin D levels and white blood cell levels checked so that my own immune system had the best chance to naturally deal with any acquired 'dis-ease'. The 'dis-ease' that I experienced in that consulting room was emotional, not physical, which was just as debilitating. Whilst conscious of my own emotional reaction, I also felt sad for that nurse, wondering what was going on for her to show so much fear.

Sometimes, it is not about the words that are said but how the person is left feeling after the interaction that will be remembered. I have come to realise that 'energy' is my first language and I understand it more than words.

On a biological level, the main difference is that bacteria are free-living cells that can live inside or outside a body, while viruses are a non-living collection of molecules that need a host to survive.

Many bacteria help us while living in our gut, digesting and helping absorption of our food. Bacteria also assist with decomposing organic materials in soil. Similarly, not all viruses are bad—we now know there are also beneficial viruses present in our gut, skin and blood that can kill undesirable bacteria and more dangerous viruses. Bacteria and viruses may not be visible to the human eye, but they are all around us in truly staggering numbers.

Viruses that are enveloped with a layer of fat (such as SARS-CoV-2 which causes COVID-19) can be more readily killed by simple hand washing, because soap disrupts this fatty layer. Viruses can't reproduce on their own (unlike bacteria) so they aren't considered 'living', but they can survive on surfaces for a varying level of time. Viruses can be quite selective about where they live and reproduce. Many don't even infect humans. Some viruses only infect bacteria, some only infect plants, and many only infect animals.

We have had viruses before and we will be exposed to them again in the future. It is the worldwide exposure that makes me wonder what else is involved, but for now I am building my own immune system in preparation. When on a plane, as part of the safety talk, they will say, 'Put on your own oxygen mask first before helping others.'

THANK YOU, VIRUS

> *'Viruses are constituent elements of life on Earth. Microwave radiation is foreign and lethal to life on Earth. It is time that humanity recognises these facts.'*
> **Arthur Firstenberg,** The Evidence Mounts

Thank you to the virus for highlighting that we only have one world with one biological system and we need each other to survive. This virus does not discriminate—it can affect us all. Most viruses have been here on this planet before we even arrived, and they will be here when we leave. As humans, we would be naive to think that we can eradicate viruses, and in trying to do so, we may end up harming more humans instead.

First, there was the computer, then we needed a program to run the computer, then came the computer virus that corrupted the program and then came the hackers. Now we have a problem because we need a computer. So, we either need to buy a new computer or find a program to fix the virus in the old computer. This is all great until another virus comes along and another fix is required. We are caught in a cycle of constantly updating our computer programs and then constantly updating the virus eliminator programs, all to supposedly keep ahead of the hackers, so that we can keep connected and working. Does this sound strangely familiar to what is happening right now? Then there is the constant update of the annual flu vaccines to ensure that our human program runs smoothly. How is that working? For me, I have had to deprogram what I put into my body, just to stay on top of my health.

Growing up, I remember being constantly sick. After leaving home, I wanted to find the cause of my sickness and not just be told, 'Take this and come back if you are not better.' At twenty-two, after watching my mother suffer and eventually die two weeks before her fiftieth birthday, I made two decisions. One, was that I was going to live beyond 50, and two, I was going to live long enough to see my grandchildren grow up. From that day my healing journey began. Doing no further harm to my body was paramount. About this time, I came across a book by Louise Hay called *You Can Heal Your Life*. After reading this book, my beliefs were really challenged and things were no longer neither black nor white.

My life took a whole new trajectory. I started to look at the impact my emotional state was having on my physical health. I even had a bet with a work colleague, saying that I would not get sick for a month, no matter who or what sickness was circulating in the office. This meant that I had to make sure that the emotional challenges from home, stayed at home. Not so easy, however I learnt not to respond to things that would previously have turned into an argument at home. I won the bet at work, however this started a whole set of new behaviours at home resulting in the loss of my own sovereignty which had unintended consequences and resulted in changed dynamics.

Just as the seemingly small change in my behaviour impacted my health and family, things were also changing at work. Their seemed to be a lot of discontent in the office, staff were leaving and not being replaced and there were discussions about moving to a new location. At this time, I was doing two jobs, office manager and accountant and the upheaval definitely added to my workload. Instead of working together as cohesive team, it became obvious to me that the litigation section did not support the commercial section and so on which impacted the productivity of the whole firm.

In hindsight, the various partners were probably all having their own challenges with the impending changes and this flowed onto their support staff. I left the firm a few years before the big changes happened and, even now, I am still in contact with colleagues from the old firm who are now also working elswehere and we reminisce and reflect on the good old times. I heard this firm got bigger, then was incorporated and many things changed which were not for the betterment of the organisation. In the 1980s, a virulent strain of capitalism came into being and took hold. Where short term profits for huge multinational entities took precedence over everything. The stock or shareholder value became more important than the safety and wellbeing of the recipients of the products. Corporate law states that it is illegal for corporate executives to put the public good before profits (shareholder value) unless required by law. There are more profits to be made preparing for war and we are in the midst of a Third World War against an invisible enemy.

As John F Kennedy said, 'If mankind does not end war, war will end mankind.' When will people realise that no-one wins fighting wars?

QUESTIONING BELIEFS

When there is light in the soul, there will be beauty in the person. When there is beauty in the person, there will be harmony in the house. When there is harmony in the house, there will be order in the nation. And when there is order in the nation, there will be peace in the world.
Chinese proverb

My wish is for everyone to find the light in their own soul.

In days gone by, it was believed that things that were written in books were written by experts who only wrote the gospel truth. However, these days there are so many experts writing books on their beliefs. Now, I am even questioning whether all the things that I have learnt about the bible are really true or only one person's interpretation. Recently, I learnt the story of Lilith and her role in religious teachings. So, I expect and hope that what is written in this book will also be questioned. All that is heard or read, is at the very least, food for further thought, whether you like it or not. Figuratively speaking, 'one size does not fit all' which explains why we often don't understand each other. In all communication there is often a difference between what the sender sends as a message and the receiver receives, which can often lead to a great deal of misunderstanding causing conflict.

I believe that many of the ways and beliefs that humanity has embraced are based on religious principles. A lecturer once told our class that, 'A fact is something that one person has convinced a group of people to believe until someone else comes along to convince that same group of people to believe something else.' To me, this makes so-called perceived facts and beliefs fluid.

A young lady recently reflected to me with astonishment on her face, 'Oh my god, this is not my belief, this belief came from my mother, and I can choose to change my beliefs.' Yes, our parents, relatives, care takers and teachers are one of our first role models and they too are a product of their own upbringings. Our beliefs are part of our automatic patterning and it is only when we become consciously aware of the automation of our beliefs that, then and only then, can we actually choose to change the beliefs that no longer serve our highest good. Life is full of changes and every moment is a new opportunity to change.

For many generations, the belief was that a woman's role was one of 'servitude' to a man—barefoot, pregnant and in the kitchen. Even the words 'wo-man' and 'fe-male', to describe the feminine sex, they have 'man' and 'male' as part of them. At birth, we start off being identified as a girl or boy. After that, the girl grows up to be a woman and a boy becomes a man. Even the words we use to describe ourselves to others reflect and reveal how we think about ourselves. It is also a belief that how we treat ourselves is often how we allow ourselves to be treated by others.

If we are respectful to ourselves and others, then there is a strong likelihood that we will also be respectful to animals and nature. While working in child protection, I was told that when I went into a family's home, take a real good look at the way the children are relating with each other and their pets. It was believed that these behaviours would more than likely give a good indication of what was happening within the person and possibly within the family.

VALUES

In our modern world, I often wonder how much we really value motherhood and children over our possessions, especially when I observe parents finding it more important to attend to their phone than playing with their children. The greatest gift we are given is being able to bring a child into the world. The responsibility that we have to our children is to nurture, love, support and teach our children what they need to know to be able to thrive in the world. Children are such a precious gift that can be harmed so easily by harsh words or actions. What I learnt is that Dr Spock, who was the child 'expert' in the 1970s, didn't know anything about my children and it was later proven that his theories were incorrect. We now know that traumatic childhood experiences, if not dealt with appropriately at the time, can resurface throughout life. Children, teenagers and young adults seem to appear so resilient however it isn't until later in life they realise how incidents that occurred in their earlier years can impact them later on in their lives.

We have all learnt things through observation, so it is really important to model the kind of behaviours that you wish to see in your children. Children are experts at mimicking what they see, even though they may not have the language or understanding. The sad thing is that, far too often, innocence, whether it be in children or adults, is exploited.

5

Council Candidate

'The planet does not need more successful people. The planet desperately needs more peacemakers, healers, restorers, storytellers and lovers of all kinds.'
Dalai Lama

STEPPING UP

On 25 September 2017, I paid a $250 nomination fee and officially put my hat in the ring as a nominee and City of Greater Geelong candidate for the Bellarine Ward. Now I was fully paid up and committed to an election which closed on Saturday 28 October 2017.

Now, let's rewind a little to where this ball started rolling. The previous council of the City of Greater Geelong Council had been dismissed, and administrators were appointed. These administrators initiated the idea of a citizen led thirty-year plan called 'Our Future' which was intended to support innovative processes which would help to shape Geelong as a clever and creative city focusing on innovation, digital technologies, education, and importantly, artists, designers and creators. This later became 'A Clever And Creative Future'.

In 2016, *The Guardian* published an article, *Story of cities #37: how radical ideas turned Curitiba into Brazil's green capital*. The article stated that, 'As an architect and mayor, Jaime Lerner led the movement that transformed Curitiba into an environmentally friendly 'laboratory for urban planning'. The secret? 'We had to move fast to avoid our own bureaucracy'.' I found this story to be inspirational and well worth reading. Curitiba, just like Geelong, was also known as a 'sleepy city'.

This was a great opportunity for myself and the residents of Geelong to be part of planning for the future of the city we call home. For the first time in my life, I felt that Geelong was planning beyond their usual three-to-four-year term of office and the community had a chance to provide their input. So, I took it upon myself to inform the businesses of what the council was planning, and the first few responses were devastating. Whilst people were happy to engage, as soon as I mentioned the council and its involvement, their body language changed. Even though they were happy to accept the brochure which explained everything, their posture indicated that this would be just another job that they did not have the energy to do.

Having been in business, I know what it feels like when you are required to conform to even more rules and regulations and asked for even more feedback, all while taking care of business. I understood that the administrators wanted to have feedback from at least 10 per cent of the population of the City of Geelong which was approximately 25,000 people at the time. I went back to the coordinators of the project to ask who their target market was. After they responded, I asked why they were not asking senior groups or children. They said that seniors and children probably would not care. How wrong they were. This response spurred me on even further as I was one of those seniors. Our seniors have learnt and experienced many things in their life which would be beneficial. Further, children are our future and we should never underestimate the wisdom of their years.

Through the various engagements around the thirty-year future planning, I met some women from Women in Local Democracy (WILD), who asked if I had considered standing for council. At that stage being a councillor had never ever been considered. However, when I saw a statement that said, 'When women support each other, incredible things happen,' I was inspired to do something different. WILD know the outcomes of this statement only too well. With principles of gender equity, diversity and active citizenship, WILD promotes women's empowerment, community participation and local political leadership.

If it were not for the support of the team at WILD, then I would never have even contemplated putting my hand forward as a candidate. I am so grateful that I had the opportunity to meet female councillors and mayors, and during our discussions was given honest and heartfelt feedback. Most of all, I have to thank my mentor, a previous mayor, for her wise, supportive and constant encouragement to keep going whilst on the campaign trail. Many times, my mentor would say that I could read between the lines of what was happening. Without her I would have given up.

Fast forward to July 2017 when the City of Greater Geelong held a candidate information session where I was informed of some of the requirements of being a councillor. This was my first lot of paperwork. Then I was introduced to workshops conducted by the Victorian Local Governance Association (VGLA), an independent organisation committed to supporting councils and councillors in good governance, and the Municipal Association of Victoria (MAV), a membership association and legislated peak body for Victoria's 79 local councils. During these informative and supportive workshops, I met Ruth McGowan OAM, an author and experienced independent political campaigner, who encouraged and supported all of the participants who came along to the meetings. Finally, the Victorian Electoral Commission (VEC) came with even more legislation and compliance rules.

As a councillor, I understood that my role would be to advocate for and on behalf of the residents of the Bellarine, as well as explaining the limitations of my role as a councillor. As a councillor the wishes of the residents must be carried out whilst also respecting the needs, culture and experiences of the residents. A councillor must also be as free as possible from any conflicts of interest when advocating or providing services for the residents.

On my candidate statement I wrote, 'Caring about the future, the people, the environment and restoring trust and integrity' as my aims.

The campaigning started even before I officially registered to run as a candidate. I had decided to run as an independent candidate and fund my own campaign, so photographs had to be taken and a statement about myself had to be created for the official flyer and registration with the Electoral Commission. Now all I needed to do was print thousands of promotional flyers, create a social media website, get help to distribute flyers, attend all interviews and community meetings, attend VGLA, MAV and VEC briefings, learn all the rules and meet as many residents as possible in a very large ward. A piece of cake, or so I thought.

During this process, I developed a deeper understanding and respect for what politicians have to go through in order to succeed. Whilst local council is the lowest tier of Government, it is definitely the one closest to the residents. Campaigning has a specific time frame, needs a budget and a good communication plan. Having a social media and public presence helps as this is definitely a time when it is important to know a lot of people. As well as the financial commitment, there is also a huge emotional and physical commitment. Then it is important to know the specific time frames, rules, regulations, guidelines etc. Finding out what skills a councillor needs, how to successfully run a campaign, learning how to refine your message and how and where you will get the best response when communicating your message. In order to be successful, you need a really good team to support you.

Whilst there was never enough time in the day, I loved the whole process. Meeting and talking to the residents and hearing their concerns, community meetings, public interviews and all the direct contact with people was a really great experience. I was shocked by the number of emails I received and in some cases I felt that some organisations were using bullying tactics in order to get votes from their particular organisation.

I have always advocated for clients in one form or another in the private and business practices I have worked in. However, the public service uses its own unique language, which I was told is termed 'public service speak'. The problem with this type of language is that the government is not actually speaking in a language that most of the public, for whom they are meant to be acting, can actually understand. Sometimes I really have to wonder if the public service really wants to actually connect with the people they are meant to be serving. By speaking to people and not over them, will always achieve a greater and more genuine connection. To be really fair, most of the politicians do not get paid enough for what they are expected to do and you have to have a pretty thick skin to be a politician. Long story short, I did not get elected.

BEHAVIOURS

It is understood that diamonds are created under pressure and pearls are created under stress. So, just like diamonds and pearls, pressure and stress can create the most beautiful things. However, being under constant pressure can cause cracks to form, and too many cracks can lead to ill health. All leaders know how to work and thrive under pressure. For a better tomorrow for ourselves, our communities and our planet, we need bold and innovative leadership.

> *'A healthy relationship doesn't drag you down. It inspires you to be better.'*
> **Mandy Hale**

Now, more than ever, it is important to hold the vibration of love, not fear. Recently, young women have shown great leadership and have been honoured for their activism against family violence and abuse. Abuse comes in many forms and all too often, bad behaviours are handed down through generations and are still being perpetuated today. The violent side of abuse has been readily identified however the more subtle forms of abuse, such as coercion, gaslighting, psychological abuse and financial control, are not as easily recognised. For someone who has experienced domestic violence, the current worldwide situation feels like 'domestic violence on steroids'.

For those of you who are like me and did not know what gaslighting meant, it has been described as a subtle form of emotional manipulation that often results in the person doubting their perception of reality which then impacts their feeling of sanity. Gaslighting has also been described as a person or a group covertly sowing seeds of doubt in a targeted individual or group. Sometimes, the very same people who profess to be concerned about the community's welfare are also the ones spreading the fear. Like everything, until you can identify what is having a negative impact on your life, there is no opportunity to change it. Many things that we do, and even say, are done automatically. Until these negative behaviours are pointed out, there is no chance of changing them. The idea is to separate the person from the behaviour. People are generally good however they can still be portraying really bad and unacceptable behaviours.

In silent acquiescence many people seem to ignore the very things that need to be identified and changed.

F.E.A.R – 'Forget Everything And Run' OR
'Face Everything And Rise'

ILLUSION OF INCLUSION

In this modern era, we want to change the wording of many things. One such word that I have heard a lot recently is 'inclusion'. What seems to be inclusive for one person is exclusive for another. The biggest assumption that is being perpetuated at this time is everybody has and uses a mobile phone. This is simply not true.

I always thought it was only the older generation that did not want to have or use a mobile phone. I was wrong. I had a conversation with a young person the other day who confirmed that she, too, did not want to have to permanently carry around her mobile phone. There are such expectations on us, created by government and business, that everybody has to download the apps or is excited about new technology. I believe that it is called FOMO (fear of missing out).

When I was very young, we did not have a telephone in our home. If we needed to make a phone call, we had to find the nearest red telephone box. Whilst this may not have been very convenient, we did survive. The biggest advantage of mobile phones is their convenience. However, now, more and more people are being diagnosed with brain cancer and there is a higher proportion of breast cancer and sterility in men, as Arthur Firstenberg revealed in his book, *The Invisible Rainbow*, which, through thorough research, highlights many of the negative consequences that our modern world technology has created on our health. If you have held a phone close to your ear for any length of time, you will notice the amount of heat that is being emitted on the adult brain, I can only imagine what this is doing to a child's brain. Be more conscious of where you are carrying your phone.

Experts have known of the detrimental health impact of electromagnetic energy for a very long time however it is the old adage of 'user beware', as Firstenberg notes.

The original mobile was the analogue 1G phone, where you could only call and text. Then we went to digital 2G which was for phone, text and minimal internet coverage only, whereas 3G included more internet network coverage. The difference between 2G, 3G, 4G and 5G is the speed and size of the network coverage. 3G works at frequencies up to 2.1 Gigahertz, 4G up to 2.5 Gigahertz and 5G can be up to 95 Gigahertz, which is thirty-eight times more powerful and dangerous than 2G, 3G and 4G. There is a lot of hype around 5G and the benefits, however it also has a greater potential to impact our health. Our mobile usage now replaces the laptop, computer and television as you can do everything on your mobile device. Years ago, my parents used to hassle me about sitting too close to the television because of the impact of radiation and yet now, we are even closer to our mobiles and at greater risk of radiation exposure.

It is great to have tools to make our lives easier however I am focused on harm reduction and if I know that something is impacting my health then I do not want to include this product in my life. The challenge is knowing what creates harm, as these days the marketing is so slick and convincing. What I have focused on in recent years is finding solutions that 'do no harm', and I wish that the companies that knowingly produce products that caused harm, would cease and desist. The sad irony is that for some companies it is more important to chase the almighty dollar than the welfare of its users. During the pandemic, some countries closed their borders, shut down businesses and called for masks and social distancing to reduce the potential of people dying and yet the products of some of the pharmaceutical companies have been known to kill and harm people for a very long time and yet they are still open for business. This does not make sense.

COERCIVE CONTROL

Community is about connecting with each other, learning and growing together and being part of something bigger. A community with a shared purpose and vision free of ads, algorithms, privacy violations, and not being part of the click-bait. According to Wikipedia, click-bait is a text or thumbnail link that is designed to attract attention and entice users to follow that link and read, view, or listen to the linked piece of online content. This is coercive control with a defining characteristic of being deceptive, misleading and typically sensationalised.

In the United Kingdom, campaigners succeeded in making coercive control a criminal offence which is a huge step forward in tackling domestic abuse. Coercive control is an act or a pattern of acts of assault, threats, humiliation and intimidation or other abuse that is used to harm, punish, or frighten their victim. Some of the actions happening worldwide right now feel like coercive control. We all deserve to be part of a community, whether local or online, that is based on principles such as compassion, caring, integrity, transparency, privacy, love and respect.

Our world is not just a series of resources. Life shouldn't just be regarded as something you can control, manipulate and manage in order to increase the power and resources of the elite that dominate our cultures and societies. It is time that indigenous cultures are respected, consulted and not exploited as they have looked after the land for centuries. It is so wrong to take advantage of people and their innocence for greed and personal gain.

Big Tech is using its power within cyberspace (the cloud) to manipulate human consciousness in a space that knows no boundaries. Big Tech's 'Orwellian behaviour' is making itself the ultimate arbiter of what we can or cannot see. Addressing the deeper social, psychological and biological issues of creating machines and apps that harvest, harbour and control our attention is a far wider issue. Unfortunately, government has no means of analysing and addressing this issue at the moment. This is exploiting a vulnerability in human psychology. When people are in fear or distracted, then they are far more manageable.

Economic malpractices seem to be out of control, or else why would more and more people be asking for so many Royal Commissions or Congressional hearings? However, these hearings and Royal Commission inquiries don't seem to lead to any real changes in regulations; maybe the odd superficial change. However, Royal Commissions do give citizens and government officials a chance to have their say. At a minimum, hearings are a chance to get public opinions and answers on record, but they often don't directly lead to any rule-changing or law-making.

Unfortunately, the short-term dopamine-driven feedback loops that have been created via social media networks are destroying the fabric of our society. They were created to help people connect more easily, and in doing so, they absorb as much of our valuable precious time and conscious attention as possible. Is this conscious theft, through manipulative mind control? I know how hard it was for me to be able to calm my mind in meditation classes as the mind never stops and it likes something to focus on, so who is really controlling the focus.

Just for a moment, stop reading and close your eyes. This immediately stops the visual distraction. Now focus on your breathing. Put one hand on the top of your chest (heart centre) and the other hand on your belly (solar plexus). Notice if you breathe into the top of your chest or your belly. Breathing into the top of your chest is shallower than breathing into your belly. Now try to breathe more deeply. As you breathe in, concentrate on directing your breath into expanding your belly. Notice your hand rise. As you breathe out, actually blow the breath out through your mouth creating a sound. Now breathe deeply into and out of your belly three times. Notice if you find yourself feeling more relaxed during this process. This is you controlling your mind and the trick is noticing the difference between conscious and unconscious mind control.

It appears that the only way people are stirred into action is by evoking their passions, loves or fears. The only ways certain individuals, businesses, corporations or countries are using to control large numbers of the population is to keep people doped up on media and nonsense. People are mindlessly ingesting information or acquiring products. At the moment, there is such a variety of information being produced at any given moment, I am not sure what to believe anymore. What is the real truth?

We are literally at a point now where tools have been created that are ripping apart the social fabric of our society. This may not be true for everyone as some people feel as though they are even more connected as a result of social media. I suppose that depends on what 'connection' means to you. For me, 'making a real connection with someone means actually being in their physical presence, face-to-face and enjoying personal interaction and conversation. Actually, having a long conversation with someone seems to be a lost art in this time of incessant busyness.

Competitiveness and cooperation are both part of nature. If a culture or a society means anything at all, it is in the values that our society promotes. If it promotes competition, then you will get a competitive culture and if our society promotes cooperation then we will get more cooperation. Consciousness is almost a neutral space, without bias, which you could take in all sorts of directions. Therefore, what values do we want our society to promote as a forefront for our culture?

Many organisations now have mission, vision and values statements. The vision is the direction in which the organisation is going and what it will do to get there. The values define what the organisation believes in and how people in the organisation are expected to behave with each other, customers, suppliers and other stakeholders.

Recently, a letter to the editor by Annie Vincent Curlewis in a local Geelong paper said:

> 'Corporate law states that it is illegal for corporate executives to put the public good before profits (shareholder value) unless required by law. For the pet food industry, there are no laws. This means pet food manufacturers usually select the cheapest ingredients, often those that have contaminants like mycotoxins at levels way beyond what is acceptable for human food production. Clearly, the welfare of animals is impacted by the food they are given. A growing number of pets are becoming sick and dying due to diseases such as megaesophagus and cancer, caused by poor quality ingredients contaminated by toxins and poisonous residues. A growing number of pets no longer live to old age. Victoria's new Animal Welfare Act must recognise that we live in a state of moral perversion. We have one moral code for the way we treat each other as human animals, and a whole other moral code for the way we treat our non-human animals. The current system allows the use of 4D (dead, diseased, down and dying) animals in the pet production chain. Stringent new animal welfare provision should provide a level playing field for pet food producers and assist producers to transition to new systems of production. The new animal welfare legislation must demand that the pet food industry be regulated and held to account by an independent body.'

How many corporations put the public good before profits?

Being a pet lover, reading the above article made me wonder about what is happening to our pets as a consequence. We don't know what we don't know.

For me, I would love to see a more loving, caring, respectful, inclusive, cooperative, compassionate society, which accepts the failing and short comings in ourselves and in others, where the overarching theme is to 'do no harm' to anyone or anything. I would like to see an end to the practice in business and society that allows for 'sacrificial lambs' as long as it helps more people than it hurts. Is knowingly hurting someone really for the greater good. Recently, it was reported that some people were experiencing side effects after receiving the COVID-19 vaccine and some suggested halting the rollout until further tests could be done to ensure it is safe for the general public. Then I heard the statement, 'Having the vaccine benefits more people than it harms. It is for the greater good.'

Many years ago, I experienced an immediate reaction to a mandatory work-related requirement to have a vaccine which made me extremely sick for months, and even years later, I still believe that my immune system remains compromised as a result.

I am not a commodity; I am a sovereign being. From birth, I do not feel like I have had a choice as to what has been put into my body or what I have been exposed to.

A recent advertisement from WorkSafe Victoria really caught my attention. It said:

> *'Let's be very clear, preventing sexual harassment is an employer's responsibility. Failing to protect workers is a crime. There are many forms of sexual harassment. These can include intrusive questions, sexualised jokes and teasing based on sexuality and gender. It's an employer's responsibility to provide a safe working environment.'*

Whilst this advert was about sexual harassment, it could apply to anything experienced in the workplace or other coercive community practices. Under the Nuremberg Code, the voluntary consent of the human subject is absolutely essential. Coercion is not consent.

The Nuremberg Medical Trial of 1946-47 revealed that German physicians conducted inhumane medical experiments on the prisoners during the Holocaust. The Nuremberg Trials were a precedent and a promise. They established that all of humanity would be guarded by an international legal shield, and that even a Head of State could be held criminally responsible and punished for aggression and crimes against humanity. However, decades after the establishment of the Nuremberg and Tokyo tribunals, the enforcement of international criminal law remains an exclusively national responsibility and the report card is appalling. Are we the victims of unethical human experiments and coerced research under national socialism?

International crimes against humanity are far too common and those responsible for the atrocities have rarely faced justice. Even today, there is huge inequity with regard to the punishment of those who have committed white collar crime and cybercrime compared to those who have perpetrated blue collar crime. How can this be a fair and just practice? Does personal autonomy really exist anymore? If this is the game of life, then I no longer choose to play by the rules, and I am becoming ever more conscious of who or what I am allowing to direct my values and beliefs. I no longer wish to be treated as a market for the direction of products, and I am aiming for a simpler life instead. Living more simply to simply live a calmer and more peaceful life.

However, I feel that the winds of change are blowing. We can create a better and more equitable world for all in which we each take personal responsibility for all of our thoughts and actions.

ENOUGH

Today I say, 'ENOUGH.'

No more of the 'give it to me now', faster, bigger, higher, more, more, more, and then even more.

Stop taking from me and others. Stop using me and my good nature for your benefit. Just because I am nice to you does not mean that you can take advantage of me. I have changed who I am because of what I have allowed to happen in my life. Yes, I am taking responsibility for my inaction and for accepting less than I deserve. I know I deserve so much more, so today I say 'enough'.

I am over the continuous invasion of my privacy. I don't want any more of your emails or so called 'notifications'. I am grateful that most of the emails have gone into spam and I regularly delete spam emails. However, now I am wondering if all the emails that I have just deleted are really spam. Were they important, or not, or another clever advertising or verbal association that has been put together to generate, attract and divert my attention by generating curiosity and/or fear? There is an old saying that 'curiosity killed the cat'.

Oh, I do get it. For you, the writers of these emails, you are just informing me or is it a deliberate and calculated diversion into what you want me to see? I am over it and I want it all to stop. I am at a place that feels like information overload and I feel as though reading one more such email will make me explode. Is it any wonder that so many people are feeling stressed with being on call 24/7, every hour of every day? How much more can we take? The pressure cooker is about to explode, and it will not be pretty. I feel as though I have been silently obedient in allowing propaganda to prevail.

For many of you, especially the younger generation, this is and has always been your world. The world of continuous distraction, keeping you forever occupied. For the new parents it has probably been a blessing, no longer hearing the words 'I'm bored' must feel like a godsend. Sometimes for parents, it can also be really frustrating when you want to divert your child's focus to something else.

Yes, I have hit breaking point, and I know from experience that if I continue on this path, I will create my own dis-ease and I definitely do not want to go there. Fear is the new contaminant and pollutant. There are enough external contaminants in this world without creating my own internal contaminant. I can't control what is external to my world, however I am totally responsible for my internal world. Oh, that sounds so wise! I have often said, 'Do what I say, which is not necessarily what I do.'

Horizontal cracks in the wall can be a sign of foundational issues, structural damage, subsidence or something else. Subsidence is the sudden sinking of a house and its foundations which tends to be caused by it having been built on a rubbish tip, or by the removal of water, oil, natural gas, or mineral resources out of the ground by pumping, fracking or mining activities.

Just like the cracks in the wall, our body, too, will show you when cracks are appearing and, when left unattended, you can sink into the abyss where the black dog hides. I have been in the abyss and it is a place that has taken me a long time to recover from. I am not just another commodity that can be exchanged for another, I am a human being who deserves to be treated with love, compassion and respect?

There is no public issue that will not come to our personal door if we do not look at the sustainability of what we are creating. Drinking green tea will not help you if the water is poisoned and the air is polluted. We cannot rely on someone else to do what we need to do.

It is my human right to feel safe in my own home, street, community and country, so why is their so much mistrust.

As a society, we can manifest global cooperation and collaboration, not isolation. We can engage with everyone in a respectful manner while focusing on all promising solutions. Through the integration of best practices, reviewing independent outcomes and using inclusive and collaborative sharing of ideas, we can create a very different, more sustainable world.

6

Social Media Impacts

'The only thing necessary for the triumph of evil is that good men do nothing.'
Edmund Burke

GOOD, BAD AND UGLY

Meaningful changes have occurred as a result of all of the social media platforms like Facebook, Snapchat, Tiktok, Pinterest, Reddit, LinkedIn, Google, Twitter, Instagram, YouTube and more. Has our innocence or naivety and the constant seeking of rewarding responses, blinded us to the flip side of this global phenomenon? It breaks my heart when I hear of anyone committing suicide as a result of cyberbullying. This is so wrong and yet so common, perpetrated every single day by a bully behind a screen.

Are you aware that when you are on social media, every single action that you take is closely monitored and recorded? They are using your psychology—everything you read, post or respond to is used to make you believe that you are being supported, where, in actual fact, they are harvesting your information for their own benefit, which, in some cases, is to your detriment. We are sold on the benefits, but it is not until we have been coerced and totally committed that we are no longer aware of the downsides.

Most users are totally unaware of the fact that they are actually being manipulated and controlled. The benefit of these platforms is that there is no longer any need for people to come together personally to interact. With Zoom and Skype, you can call anyone and see them at the same time. Many will say that we are more connected than ever and that is true, yet in many cases, these are only superficial or temporary connections.

In the documentary, *The Social Dilemma,* one of the interviewees comments that:

> *'If you want to control the population of the country, there has never been a tool as effective as Facebook. We built these things and we have a responsibility to change it (referring to the impacts of social media). The intention could be, how do we make the world better. If technology creates mass chaos, loneliness, more polarisation, more election hacking, more inability to focus on the real issue we are toast. This is checkmate on humanity.'*

The above statements are really powerful and made by the people that have worked on the inside of some of these organisations. I do not need to see the whole documentary to know that what has been said in the trailer is true. It is what I have witnessed in real life however many still seem to be blindly unaware of what is really happening, nor do they seem to care. Can we change this juggernaut into a worldwide force for good? While we like and share on social media to let others know that they are part of our lifeline and we are part of theirs. The challenge is finding a real connection when our current social distancing rules are aimed at keeping us even further apart.

Whilst pondering about the interconnectedness of so many things I came across several articles written by Amrita Grace that spoke to what I was feeling. I have highlighted some of the article below and highly recommend the full article and others that she has written.

Amrita Grace, *How Facebook has Hijacked Empathy and Compassion*, 12 October 2020
'I'm really disgusted with Facebook right now, because I've been learning about their business model, which is based in greed and manipulation. I've learned that they are collecting our data constantly, using it to modify our behaviour without us knowing it, and selling that to the highest bidder. Ignorance was bliss for a very long time, and now that I know, I can't UN-know what I now know.

'When Instagram released their new terms of service in November 2020, I read every word, and I was appalled by the liberties they are taking. They give themselves permission to acquire information such as [direct quotes from Instagram's data policy follow] 'the name of your mobile operator or ISP, language, time zone, mobile phone number, IP address, connection speed and, in some cases, information about other devices that are nearby or on your network' and 'the operating system, hardware and software versions, battery level, signal strength, available storage space, browser type, app and file names and types, and plugins' and 'access to your GPS location, camera or photos.'

Amrita Grace, *Integrity in Leadership—Why I Must Leave Facebook and Instagram*, 22 October 2020
'Once I learned about Facebook's business model, which is based in greed, manipulation, selling our data to the highest bidder, and a complete lack of ethics, I realised that I have to leave. I cannot in my integrity as a sacred feminine leader stay in support of such ugly patriarchal energies. It's not just about me personally. It's about the impact that Facebook is having on culture and society, shifting it toward angry polarisation, sensationalised fake news, and conspiracy theories that lead the gullible down deep, dark holes of distraction, despair, and addiction.

'If you want to learn more, watch The Social Dilemma *and/or read* Ten Arguments for Deleting Your Social Media Accounts Now *by Jaron Lanier. The bigger truth is that Facebook is a reflection of who we are as a society right now. A microcosm of the macrocosm. Knowing what I know, I can no longer turn a blind eye to what's happening behind the scenes as the strings are pulled this way and that by the puppet masters. Because we (the users) are the puppets.'*

Are we allowing ourselves to fall into the control of social media and the influence of artificial intelligence? Is our technology controlling us or are we using it as a tool to enhance our lives? Are we being assisted or enslaved by technology? Have we lost sight of what is really important in our lives? There are more questions than I have answers for.

Knowing all of the above does not diminish the challenges we face, nor is awareness meant to add even more weight onto our shoulders. There is nothing more important at this time than to reflect on how the things that we are doing are impacting our health and wellbeing. We create our reality through our collective imagination. Simple words have a huge impact on our nervous system as verified by a study carried out by Dr Masaru Emoto.

Are statements that are more provocative, more interesting, or is making things provocative the only way that you can get people to take notice and think differently?

The parts of the brain that are involved in speaking and understanding each other, are exactly the same part of the brain that regulates your heart, lung, immune system and so on. Humanity has a socially dependent nervous systems, and yet we live in a culture that values individual rights, freedoms and now we are also social distancing. This is a conflict, especially when we are living in an environment where we have the freedom to say what we like without taking responsibility for the negative impact that may have been caused by what we have said.

Years ago, there was a great focus on human rights. However, what never seemed to be mentioned was that there are also responsibilities that go with having rights. As I went to 'fact check' what my human rights are, I found The Victorian Charter of Human Rights and Responsibilities Act 2006, along with the Human Rights Act 2019 (Qld) and so on. To be fair, with everything that has been going on in recent times, I started to wonder what my human rights really are. After further research, I found an online campaign requesting the creation of an Australian Charter of Human Rights to ensure everyone's rights are properly protected and people have the power to hold governments to account.

I have always believed that I have had a right to privacy, however I feel that this no longer exists. Our right to privacy with regard to social media is definitely something that is debatable. Maybe finding out what my rights and responsibilities are as a citizen of Australia or, for that matter, my rights as a global human being, will be an interesting topic for another book!

7

Good Neighbours

'Your wholeness and safety lie within. Not from a partner, but this sovereignty actually leads to the deepest intimacy for you to stop using others. Let me stand on my own feet, dear Lord, and know true love.'
Tosha Silver, *True Love*

CHANGING WORLD

This is a time of great change, where on the one hand, humanity is being asked to go within and on the other hand, we are being asked to consider others and our neighbours. Our neighbours are the people sitting next to us, living next door or across the road, or in the next town, state or country. Most of the time, our vision is narrow and we only see what is before us, not really considering what we can't see further ahead. We will notice the perpetual barking of the dog next door and yet we do not hear the cry of the ill child that has been poisoned. Before any meaningful change can happen, we first have to look at ourselves and our behaviours rather than pointing the finger at what someone else is or is not doing.

When I hear that rubbish and chemicals are being dumped in the creek or ocean, I wonder if the people responsible consider the broader context of what they are doing. The creek, river and ocean are connected to people, animals and fish who rely on the water. Do the miners ever consider what is above or below the ground they are mining and the impact on aquifers? Where does the water go and who is being impacted downstream?

Many years ago, I heard that China was dumping its rubbish into the ocean and I watched a presentation by Dr Merrin Pearse showing this happening in Hong Kong. I was absolutely devastated to see that this was happening. I could only imagine what was happening to our oceans and how this would impact on the fish and other sea life. Is this another cause for the see levels rising? Dumping things in the ocean may be an 'out of sight' type of solution, however it is not morally, ethically or environmentally sustainable especially with a growing population. This is short term mentality thinking. Even Australia had to rethink what it was doing when its rubbish was no longer accepted overseas.

How and why do sinkholes happen? Did you know that anyone who owns a house on land only owns a certain depth of that land? So, I am left wondering if and when someone will be allowed to dig underneath me or my neighbours. When we do anything in some way, shape or form, our actions or inaction will impact our neighbours, no matter where they live.

For years, I have been on a personal growth journey experiencing all of life's ups and downs. Whilst the specific aspects are irrelevant the lessons have been profound. Life is like a play or a movie with you as the director. We have a dream of what we want and how we would like events to unfold. All goes well as long as the actors play the parts that you expect them to play however things tend to become unstuck when the other actors don't follow your direction. What makes it even more challenging is when you have an emotional attachment to the outcome of the play or movie.

When I was young, I did not make too many long-term plans and instead lived life in the moment. At a young age, I became a mum and things changed rapidly—all of a sudden, my life was no longer my own, nor was life just about me anymore as now there was a little person for whom I was responsible. My perspective on life became very different. Even though I was married, it did not feel as though we were making plans together. In hindsight, I was not good at reading those early signs. As a young stay-at-home mum, I got to meet my neighbours and the connection with my neighbours helped to keep me sane.

I always dreamed of what it would be like to have a family, however the reality was a very different matter. When we first came to Australia, there was only my mum, my dad and myself. Many years later, my two uncles also came to Australia, however they lived thousands of kilometres away, so I never saw them. It was in those very early years that I learnt to appreciate the value of good friends and neighbours. Immigrating to Australia and not having any extended family here, it always felt as though I was alone, even though I was blessed with wonderful friends. In those days, it was more common for women to stay at home with their young families however this is very different now. Recently, a young mum told me that she felt guilty about wanting to be a stay-at-home mum. This made me feel so extremely sad for her and the future for our children. My mother was a single mother and she had to return to work after I was born. As a result, I realised I had taken onboard deep seeded feelings of being abandoned.

In those early days, you knew the names of your neighbours, and probably most of the people in your street. Neighbours used to help and support each other out and even borrow a cup of sugar or two, if needed. There was time for chatting, looking after the kids, or the dogs and even enjoying a cup of coffee or tea together on occasions. Then, I made the decision to go to work and found that my earnings were going back to pay for childcare and vehicle costs. Years ago, it was forecast that the growth industries would be childcare, aged care and pet care. How true this was.

Somehow, the trust factor was never even considered. Nowadays, especially in the bigger cities, it is rare to even know who your neighbours are, let alone if you can trust them. It seems as though we have become so suspicious of everyone. How can we restore trust?

I am very grateful for the pandemic because it enabled me to finally meet my neighbours, know their names and even have the occasional chat and walk together. This was only due to the fact that now people were required to stay at home and work from home. It will be very interesting to see how much things change in the future.

Now is the time to have gentle and more respectful conversations and calm down a bit with regards to sharing our opinions. Too often, people are quick to respond and react to something that has triggered their emotions. As a young child, I was told to count to ten after I got angry before responding. Now, it seems like people have to get their emotions out now, without consideration or thought of the possible consequences. Find time to sit down and really listen to your inner self first. When you are with others, respect and listen to them without adding your own opinion. I believe that if someone is being hurtful, it is because they themselves are hurting. If you are that someone, comfort your own pain first, before unleashing your pain on others. Easier said than done, I know.

DO NOT DISTURB

I have often heard people say that they don't trust this or that. If this is you, then what do you trust and why? Just walk around your local street to see how many people feel as though they have to have security surveillance cameras and 'do not knock' signs at the front door. These are just a few examples of the signs I have seen:

Good Neighbours

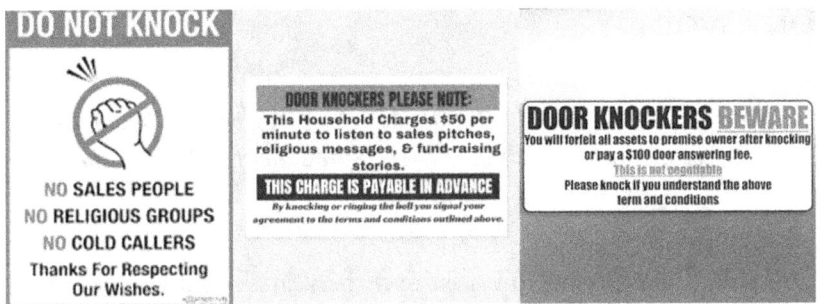

Why do people feel the need to have these signs? What has happened in our communities that has made so many people feel that this is necessary? They are another form of social distancing saying 'DO NOT DISTURB'—I do not want anyone coming to my door.

Whilst we may not be particularly keen on receiving unwanted visitors, particularly if they are trying to sell us something, the marketing we receive via our phones and computers is even more pervasive. Bring back the door knockers, as at least I can say 'no, thank you' to them. No door knocker has gotten into my home uninvited, however on the internet there is a constant uninvited invasion of my privacy. No one asked me if I wanted to be constantly bombarded with unsolicited forms of advertising. I feel as though there is someone looking over my shoulder to see what I am looking at and then the marketing starts arriving on my computer. Has this ever happened to you?

Internet marketing is like marketing on steroids.

No wonder our national debt is so high. Australia's national debt in 2019 was $25,149 dollars per person which rose dramatically in 2020. It seems like we have substituted real person to person selling for robots via our computers.

ONE WORLD

'Faith is the unshakeable knowing of the heart when nothing makes sense to the mind. Optimism is an expression of faith in action.'
Findhorn

One thing I have come to realise over the years is that you can never judge the people of any country by the actions or inaction of their leaders. We only have one world, and everything a person or country does will impact someone else and most times we don't even realise what is happening. The definition of sustainable development is the idea that human societies must live and meet their needs without compromising the ability of future generations to meet their own needs.

David Korton, an American author, wrote:

> **'Perhaps we can now recognise and accept the limits of Earth's regenerative systems and our need to help Earth heal from the damage of our recklessness. The Earth is strong, but also vulnerable. As Earth cares for us, we either care for it or bear the consequences of our recklessness. The pandemic may be seen as a not-so-subtle warning to humanity that we may be sacrificed, if necessary, to protect the health of the planet. On the path to human extinction, the most vulnerable will go first, but there will be no human winners.'**

If we would only realise that our bugs and our bees, whilst annoying at times, are also the worlds current 'canary in the coal mine'. There is much talk about global warming, however, like the unintended consequences of leather production, the world's increased reliance on technology, the proliferation of satellites sent into space and the rollout of 5G, we are wilfully blind to any of the possible consequences. Years ago, we feared the radiation, heat and destruction produced from the nuclear bomb, are our mobile phones just a mini version.

What have you done, or would you do for money?

Many years ago, I read a book called *Soul of Money* by Lynn Twist which really opened my eyes to how companies try to compensate for their mistakes with money. After reading the book, I started to question why people and companies do what they do. This was the start of my curiosity around the intention of the 'charitable gifts' of big business. Now, I am even starting to question the integral nature of philanthropy and is it all that it is portrayed to be?

A YouTube clip dated 1 May 2020 called *How Bill Gates Monopolised Global Health—His Plan to Vaccinate the World* was a real eye opener. This made me question the whole world pandemic of 2020 and how it got such a wide reach. Was it air pollution sprayed from satellites circumnavigating the world? I don't know and in time we *may* find what caused the pandemic that resulted in so many deaths and economic disaster worldwide. Or will it be another cover-up, so that the world can be vaccinated? Are we all part of the plan? Who knows! All I know is that the pandemic has created a lot of fear and at times extreme panic. What would the truth create?

Back to philanthropy, most of us have donated funds to people and charities on occasion, which we believed were unconditional and with the purest of intent. Or maybe not so totally pure if it was used to get a tax deduction. In January 2020, millions of dollars were raised for the Trustee for New South Wales Rural Fire Services and Brigades Donations Fund and wildfire relief. This shows how generous people are and what is possible in times of emergency. I truly hope that these funds went to where they were intended to go.

Many donations were given anonymously, whereas some donors wanted accolades, however there was also an attempt at guilt-tripping people into donating which is morally wrong and should not be tolerated. Is this really the Australian way to show us how much money you have got and how much you are prepared to give or else you will be judged and shamed? From my experience, I have seen so many amazing people doing amazing things, who get on with what needs to be done and these people are the heroes and the quiet achievers.

The way people come together in times of crisis again shows what good neighbours do for each other and in these cases, you may never know who the person is that has provided the support.

GROWING A BETTER FUTURE

I have a dream to celebrate the birth of each child worldwide by planting a tree. To grow a future that values all life, that is sustainable, loving, caring and compassionate. I believe that the world has more than enough of all that we need, however the biggest problem is that our needs are not equally distributed throughout the world. In reality, we need very little to survive, however it is greed and desire that destroy the real wealth of humanity. Bring back gratitude for blessings and all that we already have and appreciate and simply say 'thank you'.

At the time of reading Lynne Twist's *Soul of Money,* as mentioned above, I did not fully understand what the author was referring to, but now I understand better. It is not about how much money you have or the money that is the problem; it is where and how the money is spent and what you do with what you have got. There is a myth that has been circulating for far too long which says, 'The more money you have the more of a difference you can make.' I would like to suggest a new reality: 'There are many things you can do without money however you cannot do anything without people.' It is time that we honour all people for their contributions to this wonderful world.

This came from an anonymous source and they are great principles to live by:

- Honour yourself and live with integrity;
- Value integrity and recognise who you are and the values that you aspire to;
- Be true to yourself and stay true to your beliefs;
- Be sure to do right by others and always take the high ground;
- Keep good company;
- Be confident and do what is right;
- Be honest and transparent;
- Honour your word, to yourself and to others; and
- Accept personal responsibility.

8

Respecting Others

CHANGE IS INEVITABLE

'Change happens when the pain of staying the same is greater than the pain of change.'
Tony Robbins

The pandemic highlighted which services are classified as essential. The Essential Services Act 1981 (SA) defines 'essential services' as a service (whether provided by a public or private undertaking) without which the safety, health or welfare of the community or a section of the community would be endangered or seriously prejudiced.

During the health crisis, services such as nurses, doctors, ambulance workers, cleaners, teachers, childcare, aged care, supermarkets, couriers, post office and other food suppliers were brought to the fore and really highlighted as 'essential services'. Women, especially mothers, have been providing the majority of the services identified as 'essential' for a very long time and yet this was the first time in my lifetime that these services were recognised as essential. At the forefront of all these services was hygiene. What is essential for some may be mere survival for others.

AFRICAN NEIGHBOURS

In October 2010 I went on a four-week tour of Kenya. In hindsight, this was not a holiday it was a healing journey. I had not realised, until recently, that the reflections of my time in Kenya were so profound that they have entered many of my conversations since.

A seemingly simple question often started the conversation ball rolling: 'Why do you call our country (Kenya) developing and your country (Australia) developed?'

This single insightful question initiated many discussions, firstly with a fellow travelling companion and then on my return home with people from the wider community. Reflecting on this question brought about so much more awareness and gratitude for where I live and what I am privileged to have today. It is so easy to take many of the things that are provided to us for granted. The following is not a travel guide but a reflection from the journey itself. I hope you will find something that will inspire your life's journey.

Why did I go to Africa, and specifically to Kenya? Whilst I had previously travelled to Asia and Europe, Africa never quite made it onto my bucket list. At this particular time in my life, I was desperately trying to make sense of my life and looking for meaning. This had been a really traumatic time; I was bleeding money and the sharks were circling.

I needed to re-evaluate and 'restart' my life. An acquaintance was planning a 'Heart and Evolution Tour' into Kenya and she asked if I wanted to go with her. I am someone who believes that if I am meant to do something then I will get signs—well, the signs came. Firstly, people I met started to talk about their trip to Kenya and then there was a competition to win two tickets to a show about Africa. I don't usually enter competitions, but this time I did, and to cut a long story short, I won. That was it; I had to find a way to go on this all-inclusive trip to Kenya. A few days before I was due to fly out, I found out that I was the only person on the tour. I took a deep breath and decided that whatever happens it was meant to be. A test of ultimate trust.

Until the tour started, I had no idea that my tour guide was not a professional travel agent, although fortunately she was very organised, had been to Kenya before, and all of what I was promised in my itinerary, I received and more.

The first couple of days we spent on and off planes and in airports before our final arrival at Nairobi, the capital of Kenya, where we were greeted by a traditionally dressed Maasai warrior with a large knife hanging from his hip. At that very moment I felt very vulnerable and wondering what the hell I had gotten myself into. All of a sudden, I felt very reliant on my tour guide and, in reality, I was far too tired to really care as I badly needed sleep. My vulnerability was exposed. I have done a fair amount of travelling to many countries, however none has had a more profound effect on my life than Kenya. I took a risk and was rewarded in ways I could never have imagined.

WORLD WAR III—UNSEEN ENEMY

I have always felt very privileged to be living in Australia and am grateful to my parents for making that supreme sacrifice to migrate here. Travelling to Asia made me even more appreciative of my little three-bedroom, one-bathroom house, which was not very fancy, but it was my home and palace.

Fast forward fifty years and I have again been reminded of how grateful I am to be living in Australia. This gratitude is due to the fact that Australia, as a whole, has had a very low number of deaths or sickness from the virus that has invaded the world. Compared to many other countries, we have been very lucky. However, if you have been one of those families who has lost a loved one, that is one death too many.

What I have specifically noticed is the fear that is generated by all the media reporting. Personally, I am grateful to the reporters for collating all the facts for those who need to know; however, as an empath and a worry wart, I need to turn off and tune out. This makes it really hard when rules of what you can and can't do locally, state-wide and nationally are changing almost daily. The worldwide pandemic has created so many changes for so many people, businesses, communities and nations as a whole. Thinking about the global impact, it is very hard to even comprehend, however when my community was asked to go into lockdown and we were asked to isolate, the whole situation became personal and local.

Lockdown meant you were only allowed to leave home for essential reasons, such as work, exercise, grocery shopping or medical appointments. If you were in the vulnerable category, over sixty-five years of age, or immune-compromised, then it was recommended that you do not leave home at all. Businesses were asked to shut their doors, employees were asked to work from home where possible and a new hygiene regime was put in place. The key messages were, stay safe, wash hands regularly, keep one-and-a-half metres apart and socially isolate.

Being in virtual shutdown has given me lots of time to reflect on what really matters in my life. I can only imagine how these very unusual times have impacted your life. What has really stood out for me is what is classified as essential services and the number of times that our leaders and other people have said 'thank you' to the essential service workers and acknowledged the services that they have provided. Mothers and fathers have provided those same services every single day as part of normal life which have mostly been taken for granted. What has not been identified is that the lack of physical touch, fear and anxiety can be more toxic than any virus.

NEEDS

What are you connected to and disconnected from? Do you really feel as though you have the supports that you really need? Are you being empowered or dis-empowered? This is the time to wake up to the fact that we are all connected to the human family whether directly or indirectly and we all need each other in one way or another.

Let's all pull together to build a new and stronger foundation for our future. One of the basics that is really needed in our lives is to get enough sleep. With enough sleep, your energy will be recharged to be fully present for what you need to do the next morning. Sleep is not just about restoring your physical energy; it is also about your emotional energy. In these unprecedented times, our brains are constantly firing to take in the ever-evolving changes. We are in hyper drive and therefore it is even more important to find a way to fully shut off. How do you switch off and fully recharge? Even our mobile phones require regular charging to keep going. What you think of last thing at night stays with you, so it is important to think of something positive before you go to sleep for sweet dreams.

Whilst our bodies need adequate sleep, we also need water. Since our bodies are 70 per cent water, we cannot survive for more than a few days without water. Adequately hydrating yourself on a daily basis is vital to keeping your body functioning properly. Not having enough water and becoming dehydrated may create a barrier to good sleep. At the same time, too much water before bed may or will, as in my case, cause sleep interruptions.

There is a great deal of difference between our wants and our needs. The hardest thing is to separate a 'need' from a 'want'. If you want it then you probably don't need it.

BREAKING THE CYCLE OF POVERTY

I always wondered why poverty exists in both wealthier and poorer countries. A social enterprise can usher in a new kind of capitalism, one that values altruism and generosity just as much as it does financial gain, and in doing so create a 'World of Three Zeros': zero poverty, zero unemployment and net zero carbon emissions. This was the vision of Grameen Bank founder and Nobel Peace Prize winner, Professor Muhammad Yunus. Mohammad Yunus set up the Grameen Bank in Bangladesh in the 1970s with such a vision in order to support the poor. While Yunus was teaching traditional economics at university, he saw people outside the university dying from starvation. Yunus realised that clearly there was a difference between the theory that he was teaching and real-life practice. Professor Yunus created a system that unlocked people's potential allowing people to come out of poverty. Yet fast forward fifty years and clearly things have not changed. Hopefully, the health and economic crisis of 2020/21 will allow us all to rethink, reset and re-evaluate our social structures and lifestyles to create positive change.

A possible resurgence of The Co-operative Group retail company, established in 1844 in the United Kingdom, may be a possibility. This cooperative group was created to protect the livelihoods of entrepreneurs who produced high quality, sustainable products from larger industries producing poor quality less expensive mass-produced goods. Also, when mass production started, larger industries relied on unfair labour practices, which in some places still continue today. For those who have never heard of the co-operative, it is a democratic organisation, owned and controlled by its members for a common benefit. Co-operatives are traditionally based on the values of self-help, self-responsibility, equality and solidarity. The members of the co-operatives share in the group's investment and operational risks and losses as well the benefits.

Usually, co-operatives are based on specific values. They operate according to specific principles and, at the heart of it all, share a concern for people over profits. However, in saying that, I will put my business hat on and acknowledge that when organisations are solely relying on volunteers to do their core business, that is not respecting or valuing their workforce. I have a belief that nobody would be unemployed or poor if there was a more equal distribution of income.

DOING THINGS DIFFERENTLY

Things are changing and people are doing things differently. I have personally invested in a community owned renewable energy project that has installed solar panels on an aged care centre. While not often mentioned, I am pleased to say that there are many co-ops existing today and in my local community there is a housing co-op and the rapidly growing Wathaurong Aboriginal Cooperative. Maybe you could think of other social businesses or co-ops that exist in your area. Now is the time to support good quality, environmentally friendly, fair trade sustainable businesses.

Years ago, I applied for a position with a not-for-profit charitable organisation. When I was being interviewed for the job, I was told, 'We can't afford to pay you very much because we are a charitable organisation.' I responded by saying that I did not see this charitable organisation as any different to a for-profit organisation. The only difference between a not-for-profit and a for-profit organisation is where the profits go. As I saw it, the more efficiently that this charity was operating then the more people it could support. It was obviously a very different way of thinking and I got the job. I acknowledge that we all have different educational qualifications, abilities and work experiences. On top of that, I acknowledge that all roles and jobs have different responsibilities and pressures, therefore these variances should be remunerated differently.

During difficult financial times, it is the businesses with minimal overheads that seem to survive. Locally, there is a family-owned and operated service station which is doing a roaring trade and keeping the fuel price low. In contrast, the larger fuel companies that have a more corporate structure with directors, CEO and middle management who all need to be paid, will find it more difficult to retain reasonable profits if they have to compete with the lower fuel prices. I have often believed that there are too many businesses that have too many highly paid executives and not enough fairly paid workers or investors.

9

Balancing Priorities

OPTIONS

Whilst at university, I was involved in conducting statistical research as part of my coursework to obtain my qualifications. Research becomes very time-consuming when you look into all sides of the brief. A colleague suggested that next time I should just ask my lecturer what they wanted to prove by doing the research and then find the corresponding research to validate that. For my colleague it was all about doing the minimal amount of work to achieve the eventual goal, which was to find a well-paid job after qualifying. My colleague had a different attitude to study than I did, however, in hindsight, I realised that universities were actually using students to do unpaid research work. For that matter, social media giants are freely harvesting our information every day to sell to the highest bidder. In all fairness, there are some research companies who are prepared to pay people for their opinions.

Knowledge is power and those with the knowledge are the ones who have the power. Previously it was said that it is not what you know but who you know. Now, more than ever, what you know will give you the power to be more independent. In 2009, I voluntarily worked for No Interest Loan Scheme (NILS), a micro-financing organisation that makes small zero-interest loans to the impoverished without requiring them to provide any security. This provides a way for people to get away from the cash converters, payday lenders and other short-term lenders that charge exorbitantly high interest for the privilege of accessing their money.

NILS provided individuals and families on low incomes with access to safe, fair and affordable credit. It was based on a similar principal as the Grameen Bank. The Grameen Bank was founded in 1983 in Bangladesh by Muhammad Yunus to fight poverty. Grameen's revolutionary model empowers the poor, particularly women, to take charge of their own futures and reach their full potential. In 2020, the Grameen Bank launched in Australia. Grameen Australia is part of the Grameen family of global organisations and is a not-for-profit purpose driven charitable organisation registered with the Australian Charities and Not-For-Profits Commission (ACNC).

Grameen lends small amounts of money as working capital, called microfinance, to individuals or a group of borrowers, who are collectively responsible for each repaying their loans. This is called social collateral. To support this, they are offered mentoring, training and business education. Unlike transnational banking, the model has a built-in savings component which requires clients to save and promotes asset building. The Grameen model is intended to become a self-sustaining social business in Australia where 100 per cent of the capital invested gets paid back, and all profits get reinvested to help more borrowers out of hardship to live fuller lives. Micro-financing has been proven to have a wider social impact by lending money to women who can then, not only support themselves, but their children, families and communities.

ADDICTION

I have to confess that I had an addiction to video games which was impacting my life and I needed to find a way to break free. The first step to changing any addictive habit, is to acknowledge the addiction. How could the simple act of playing a game cause any problems? Yes, gaming did consume a lot of my time, however I could control it, or so I thought. It wasn't like being addicted to drugs, alcohol, work or social media. To be honest, for a very long time I was not prepared to admit that I had a problem until I found that I was having trouble focusing on the things I needed to do, like finish this book.

So, I started looking for help and was really surprised at how much information I found on the internet related to gaming addiction. Apparently, video gaming and addictive drugs affect the brain in the same way through the release of dopamine. This made me reflect on the rewards of gaming and social media interactions. Playing games was a great way to numb out. Consistently improving my gaming scores made me feel good and kept me engaged. I wasn't hurting anyone but me.

Dopamine is a chemical in our brain linked to our motivation to do things and can become activated when something good happens or we get and feel rewarded. When dopamine is released in large amounts it can lead to addictions. According to the World Health Organisation (WHO), a video game addiction is a legitimate mental health disorder. The media are constantly reporting that there is a mental health crisis and a crisis for some is an opportunity for others. At the moment, our world and humanity seem to be swinging from one crisis to another. The challenge will be figuring out what crisis is of highest importance. What is of highest importance to our government may not be of the same importance for the individual.

Reporter Kristy Grant wrote an article dated 3 January 2020 called *Dopamine fast: The hunger and boredom were intense.* The first sentence in this article was, *'Dopamine fasting is a lifestyle trend popular in the world's tech centre Silicon Valley which involves cutting yourself off from almost all stimulation for 24 hours.'* It is believed that dopamine fasting can reset the mind, improve focus, productivity and happiness. So, why aren't we all doing a dopamine fast?

We build a tolerance to dopamine quick hits from things like social media, pornography, shopping, gaming and junk food. The rules for 'fasting' are, no TV, internet, phones, reading, music, or podcasts, no sexual activity, no alcohol or caffeine, limited talking, no eating and drinking only water, for a 24-hour period. The fasting rules are simple as you can drink only water (no food), meditate, hand write (no computers), do light exercises or go for a walk (avoiding busy streets). I have done a food fast and a ten-day Vipassana silent retreat, which was very challenging. At the retreat there was no talking, no reading, no music, minimal exercise and good vegetarian food for ten days and nights. The Vipassana meditation is a way of self-transformation through self-observation and well worth the effort however I would suggest starting with the three-day meditation. Whilst I am not attached to my phone, and often leave home without it, even I would find Silicon Valley type of dopamine fasting difficult.

> *'It allows you to reflect and look at the bigger picture, to reassess.'*
> **James Sinka, entrepreneur and fasting advocate**

Maybe the key to happiness is going back to the basics and avoiding, or at least really minimising the dopamine 'quick hits'. How would you go with the Silicon Valley dopamine fast?

In 1986, Steven King released the horror movie, *It*. Maybe the information technology movement is the real horror movie of the modern era. Like most things, the tools that help and support our lives are great, however, for many people, technology has taken over and totally consumed their lives. What is even sadder is that there are quite a few people I know who will not answer their phone for fear of being confronted by a smooth-talking scammer. When government agencies and businesses can get hacked, then what chance do the rest of us have?

Russian physiologist Ivan Pavlov was successful in conducting a psychological experiment that proved he could condition his dog to salivate in expectation of food when he rang a bell. Just like Pavlov's dog, have people been classically conditioned by all of the perpetual buzzing, pinging and ringing of their mobile phones and their electronic devices. Have we been conditioned to respond to the constant bells and whistles or are we in control? We are human beings, not computers, and being on call 24/7 creates so much more stress in our lives. It is ridiculous to be constantly bombarded with scams, spams, surveys, reminders, offers of money, love, constant advertisements with discounts, retail offers and no I don't want to download your app. When does it stop? Bring back some sanity, turn off your mobile phone and provide only snail mail contact details to anyone other than your inner circle. Some people still don't realise that you cannot send a text message to a landline phone. I can guarantee you that there are many people who do not want to be permanently connected to their mobile phone.

SMART TOWN

A few years ago, I decided to drive with a friend from Melbourne to Darwin, a 3,740-kilometre journey through the centre of Australia. It was an amazing trip that made me realise what a big and truly amazing country Australia really is. The landscape which was so different to anything I had ever experienced before and there was clean unpolluted air. At night, it felt as though you could almost touch the stars that shone so brightly. I can now understand why our indigenous people and the grey nomads want to go north and live simply on the land without the trappings of modern life.

During our travels, we experienced many amazing towns and Coober Pedy was one such town which made me realise that the residents were very smart. Coober Pedy is known as an opal mining town and nearly 80 per cent of the population live underground. When these residents do renovations in their underground homes, there is a good chance that they make more money from the opals they find, than what they spend on renovations. A novel thought. The landscape in this town is so unusual that it was used in the film, *Mad Max: Beyond Thunderdome*.

The most profound realisation that impacted me about Coober Pedy was in relation to the mounds of dirt everywhere, as well as all the large rusting machines. When I asked our tour guide and local resident about these machines, he said that years ago, the local opal miners were offered these amazing machines that would increase the productivity of their opal mines. What the miners soon found out was that the machines and diesel were costing them more than they were earning from the extra opal mining. So, they decide to return to their previous mining practice and left the machines where they stood. Is there something that we could all learn from this tiny town?

CHOICES AND CHANGES

> *'According to the statistics in 2008 the national debt per person was $5,777 and in 2018 it was $23,512.'*
> **Country Economy**

> *'In 2015-16, around three quarters (74%) of households held debt, and the average household debt of all households was $168,600. The most common form of debt was credit card debt, held by 55% of households, followed by home loans (34%) and student loans (17%).'*
> **ABS**

No wonder so many people are so stressed out and believe that they can't afford to buy a house. The stimulus package given by the government in 2008 helped the economy through the financial crises of 2008 and ten years later the spending was nearly five times more. It will be interesting to see what a difference the government stimulus in 2020/21 will make to the future national debt.

As can be seen by the rise of the Australian national debt from 2008 to 2018, we must be a wealthy country, in which case, why are so many people struggling to pay their debts? Yet, whenever people are asked, they say they can't afford to do certain things and yet can afford to do many other things. It is all relative and it all comes down to that six-letter word: 'choice'. We choose what we can and can't afford. Never before in history has it been more important to consider all that we are doing, all of our actions or inaction. What we do now will determine the impact that our choices have on our personal, business, community and the environment.

Many wonderful people have started organisations and support groups with the intention of doing much-needed work, however sometimes it seems more about raising the money than providing the service that was intended to be provided. Rotary International is an international service organisation, founded by Paul P Harris in 1905, whose stated purpose was to bring together business and professional leaders in order to provide humanitarian service and promote goodwill and peace around the world. It is a non-political and non-religious organisation open to all.

The Hunger Project, founded in 1977 by John Denver, Werner Erhard and Robert W Fuller, is an organisation committed to the sustainable end to world hunger and the Australia website states, 'Make the impossible possible and end hunger by 2030.' It is now over fifty years since this organisation was founded, and yet has anything really changed or is the gap between the haves and have nots even wider? There are sufficient resources in our world to support everyone however the problem is the inequity of distribution, not to mention the waste.

From Impossible to Possible, a two-minute YouTube video clip on The Hunger Project Australia website, shows the power of the people and what can be achieved. After the clip, The Hunger Project published a statement saying:

> *'People are extraordinary. Humanity has achieved incredible feats. With resilience, courage, ingenuity and creativity, we can make the impossible possible. Together, we can end world hunger. World hunger is a complex problem, but it is not a hopeless problem. Pioneering, innovative work is being done worldwide. In the last 25 years, extreme poverty has nearly been cut in half. We can finish this. Let's make history together and end world hunger by 2030.'*

I believe that humanity has the ability to change anything, however, first, we have to get out of the trance that we are in. The trance of consumption. Are we addicted to consumption and ignoring the simple pleasures of life? We do have a choice and we can implement change, but first we have to stop and open our eyes to see what is really going on. To see how we are being manipulated and what we, as a society, have believed to be true. Is it really true? To be quite frank, I don't know what is true anymore what is right or wrong. What really matters is what we are prepared to do to change that which no longer serves the greater good.

10

Self-Care—Others— Me or We

SELF CARE

> *'When a woman heals herself, she heals those who came before her and those who come after her.'*
> **Christiane Northrup**

I believe that there has never been a more important time in history than the present to heal ourselves, and in doing so, we will indirectly heal our planet. It all starts with us. In ancient times, women were deeply revered and held in high regard as leaders, shamans, warriors, healers and mothers in their societies. A woman's womb carries the creation of life, enormous healing potential, ions of wisdom and the ability to connect to inter dimensional knowing. I believe that we all have this psychic ability however over time this has been forgotten or simply no longer trusted. We have become disconnected and no longer listening to the wisdom of our inner knowing. Instead, many people are relying on what the outer world is telling us.

There is outdated thinking that says that it is better to take care of others than ourselves. It is time to change our thinking if we want to create a different outcome. If you have ever been on an aeroplane, the safety instructions say that it is essential to put your own oxygen mask on first before assisting anyone else. However, after doing so much personal work, I have come to realise that it is much easier to look after someone else than to have a long, cold, hard look at yourself. When you are pointing the finger, with thumb and forefinger pointing forward, the other three fingers are pointing backwards at you. What you see in someone else is only a reflection of yourself, as if you were looking in the mirror.

RUNNING ON EMPTY

The truth is, when you are running on empty, you can't support anyone else. When you have nothing to give, you simply have absolutely nothing to give. This is what I experienced as burnout. In a car you have a fuel gauge which tells you how much fuel is in the petrol or gas tank. The problem is I do not know anyone with a personal fuel gauge. So, how would anyone know when they are nearing empty? In hindsight, my body did tell me, but I ignored the signs, popped another pill and did even more exercise to 'hopefully' make myself stronger and more resilient. I feel that today's society is on a similar trajectory to major mass burnout.

Our modern world is obsessed with busyness. Many of us run around from here to there, in circles but not really getting anywhere, doing this and that, with no time to be still. I wonder if all that activity is really allowing us to lead fulfilling and productive lives. Just *stop* for a few moments and reflect. If you are reading this and it resonates with you, then I know that you, too, are searching for answers. I'm sorry, but I do not have the answers for you and your life as this is your journey. Hopefully, what I have learnt can provide you with another way of looking at aspects of your life. What I do know for sure is that your life is your life and nobody else can live it but you.

This may sound like common sense, however many of us hand our lives over to others to tell us what to do.

I wish I could be the one to give you the answers that you are looking for, however I am not you and only you are the one who knows exactly what you need. Are you ready to stop long enough to ask yourself what you need and then be patient enough to wait for the answer? The answer will come; the trick is to be patient enough and stay quiet enough to hear it. Divine timing!

I am sure you have heard the saying, 'When the pupil is ready to learn, the teacher will arrive.'

Maybe the truth is that we need to slow things down. The other day I heard someone say, 'You talk too fast, I can't understand what you are saying.' Often, I have heard people talk over one another and I wondered if anyone really heard what the other person was saying. This is not being respectful.

Emmi Mutale, a deeply intuitive energy medicine practitioner recently wrote an article explaining her journey in which she stated:

> *'A big part of this shift is that we are nearing the end of the era of patriarchy—an era that saw women suppressed, silenced, ridiculed and punished and that has led to deep trauma and wounding in the collective consciousness for both women and men. As we move closer to fifth dimensional reality—one that is based on love, collaboration and compassion—we are also awakening to the importance of the dance between the sacred feminine and the sacred masculine. I spent years leading my life from a predominantly masculine energy, setting ambitious goals, taking constant action, ticking off to do lists and using my rational mind to solve problems and come up with solutions. I ignored my growing tiredness, brushed aside the signs my body was giving*

me, buried my emotions deep inside and pushed through pain and illness. Until one day, the walls I'd built around me came crashing down and I found myself wailing on my bathroom floor, looking for a way out. A permanent way out. You see, in my desire to climb the career ladder and succeed according to what I then believed to be 'success,' I had completely ignored my feminine side. That side that wanted to invite in delicious, sacred pauses, take moments of rest in the middle of the day, listen to the wisdom of my body and flow according to my natural rhythms and allow my inner knowing to guide me.'

What I have learnt through my own reflection is just how similar our personal experiences are. It is only when our personal experiences are shared that we realise what Emmi has reflected is like a mirror for our own life experiences. When things of the flesh no longer fulfil you, the type of things that are here today and gone tomorrow, then going within yourself to the core of who you are, your spirit, the part of you that has never left you and honouring that side, this will be everlasting.

The never-ending to-do list is the greatest distraction that will keep you going to a point. When you reach that point in your life where you are still wondering when or what you need to do to find happiness, contentment, peace or whatever it is for you, then be prepared to make the time for these inner reflections.

INNER REFLECTION

Too many times, we look outside of ourselves to receive the love that we most need to give to ourselves. We measure our self-worth by how much we are loved and valued by those around us, how many Facebook or other social media friends we have or the likes we get to our posts. It is what we think and believe about ourselves that often has the most impact on the way we feel about ourselves and our self-worth.

The love we really need, and the answers to what we most need, come from within. The trick is to be still and listen. Is your own internal voice louder than the external voices? More importantly, what are you saying or believing about yourself? Nobody can hurt you more than you can hurt yourself.

When you love and care for yourself, you are effectively loving and caring for everything and everyone, not the other way around. We can do this by awakening our own sacred divine feminine, the one which resides within each of us, no matter our gender. We are both masculine and feminine however we major in one and minor in the other. At this moment in time, I feel that our masculine and feminine energies are at war and to find peace, we must balance and accept both within us.

> *'If women ran the world, we wouldn't have wars. Just intense negotiations every twenty-eight days.'*
> **Robin Williams**

It requires a paradigm shift from the current patriarchal rule to honouring and respecting the feminine within everything: whether we are male, female or non-binary; the earth and all her elements and inhabitants; each other, regardless of race, gender, economic status, religion or lifestyle. The masculine and the feminine each have very different qualities and it is the acceptance, appreciation and integration of both that will create harmony. It is about finding the love and respect for the uniqueness of ourselves and each other. The reality is, if you don't love yourself unconditionally, how can you expect someone else to love you?

PAINFUL

> *'The children of the future
> will be dead before their parents.'*
> **Beth Green**

When that particular statement was made in a recent podcast, it stopped me in my tracks. I was absolutely horrified at that thought that I didn't even hear much of the podcast after that statement. Nearly twenty-five years earlier, I remembered a colleague saying something similar, 'The parents of the future will lose their children, our way of communicating will be very different and you will know if people are lying.'

I must admit, at the time, I was a bit sceptical about what my colleague had said, however I did think it would be great to know if someone was lying. No more deception. I thought it would be cool to use telepathy to communicate. There is no way that twenty-five years ago I could have even imagined social media or any of the other forms of communication that are being used today.

Nor would I have wanted to even think about losing a child. Whilst I have not actually lost a child through death, which would be devastating, the most painful thing in my life was not my divorce, it was losing my children and grandchildren. I have not seen my children or grandchildren for a very long time and this alienation has been my most painful experience. What gives me hope is that maybe one day this will change.

I have had to learn to love my children and grandchildren from a distance and accept what is. I have had to learn not to blame myself as that does not change anything. I have had to learn that it is OK to be too much and that I have a right to be who I am and not have to change to please others. I have learnt that no matter what I have done or how much I have sacrificed and changed, it has not been enough to please others. I have given enough and now it is time to receive. Through this pain, I have had to learn to love all of who I am and own my own story without guilt or shame.

SCREAMING INTERNALLY

Have you ever watched a young child trying to express themselves to the adults around them, feeling so frustrated that they are not being understood, or that the adults don't seem to care? Then someone says to them that they are 'telling stories' and brushes them off. I have seen the humiliation on that child's face because, to her, she was not telling a story; she did not have the words or knowledge to fully explain what she was trying to convey. Someone said to me many years ago that a child is a young adult without the adult experiences or the vocabulary to express themselves.

Is it any wonder then that a two-year-old child seems to have so many tantrums? They must feel so frustrated because they have to keep repeating what they are saying so that they can be understood. Whilst a two-year-old may do a lot more external screaming, an older child may turn their frustration inward because of their inability to express themselves, so that the adults around them can appropriately tend to their needs. Children have very good instincts and know what does not feel right. Yet, more often than not, adults seem to dismiss their children's natural, instinctual responses by telling them that everything is alright. This creates great confusion for these children, and they begin to doubt their natural feelings, hence shut down their intuitive abilities.

Childhood abuse can have a child screaming inside because they cannot understand why they feel so bad, and yet everyone involved seems to be laughing and joking. It would be extremely hard for a child to express their feelings when they have not learnt the words that explain the way they are feeling. Even adults seem to have trouble explaining how they feel at times. Any in-depth conversations are seemingly too hard and yet are needed more than ever these days. Many people seem to be excellent at small talk involving gossip or the weather, however deeper conversations are seen as daunting and become out of bounds: the no-go zone. The challenge is to find the balance between too much mindless chatter or complete silence. Find time to stop, reflect and consciously decide on how things and conversations can be done differently.

It seems like everybody is talking and nobody is really listening or are there so many distractions demanding our attention that we don't have the time to give our full attention to anyone or really listen to what they are saying. As a society, we have lost the ability to 'debate', or at least have a robust discussion. When I was young, I really enjoyed being part of the debating team at school. Debates involved two teams of students discussing a chosen topic. One team discussed one point of view and the other team was asked to express an alternate point of view on the same topic. In other words, seeing another person's point of view.

Debating is a way of expressing your point of view on a particular topic. Debating allowed me to look at topics from another person's perspective, rather than just my own. The challenge is keeping emotion out of the debate when different points of view are being expressed. The difference between a discussion and an argument is an emotional reaction. What I have observed, especially around topics which were previously hidden behind closed doors, like family violence and sexual abuse, is the number of emotional reactions being evoked.

GENERATIONAL DIFFERENCES

When I was young, I could not wait to grow up and go out into the world to do what I wanted when I wanted to do it. However, I soon learnt that reality was very different. I learnt that what I did could impact others and that their actions could impact my way of life and thinking. This is not unique to our current time, as I remember my parents and grandparents saying how different things were in their day compared to today. I am sure that the following generations will probably say the same.

I would like to live in a world where all women are respected and honoured. Small acts towards change are the greatest way to enact change. It is about being the change that you want to see in the world. Model the behaviour you want to see.

Once when working with children there was a programme called *Catch Them Doing Good* which involved praising children when they have done something good, instead of focusing on what they have done wrong. Even if children were doing something incorrectly, let them know what you want them to do. I was told that, to support a child's self-esteem and self--worth, it was important to give three compliments for every one reprimand. To achieve this takes real focus. It is also important to separate the person from the action; in other words, the behaviour was bad, not the person doing the behaviour. In many ways, I have always believed that it is more important to teach children EQ (emotional quotient, or emotional intelligence) than focusing on their IQ (intellectual quotient). Developing strong self-worth and self-esteem is important for all of us as it impacts mental health, wellbeing, behaviours, boundaries and how we relate to others.

STORIES

The foundation of all learning begins at home, and there is a dimension of consciousness in all of us that we can discover and access. In other words, discovering the ability to be aware of when we have a thought and then be a witness to our thoughts. Our consciousness is often described as the thinking mind, however being conscious can even be the simple act of stopping what you are doing and simply being present. Being present does not require any thinking. By simply being in the present moment, becoming aware and noticing our surroundings like sounds, smells, sensations, feelings, memories as well as our thoughts. This observation can be like watching a movie. I am not my thoughts and who I am is not derived from my thoughts. Our identities are defined by what we think about ourselves. We are our own worst enemy and nobody can make us feel any worse than what we say about ourselves.

What story have you created about yourself? Most importantly, is that the real truth of who you are? Have we allowed ourselves to be shaped by the collective consciousness in order to be accepted? What happens when we no longer feel accepted? Thoughts about ourselves are like a viral infection experienced on a mental level, both individually or as a collective. The challenge is to become aware of when you have allowed yourself to be taken over by the collective consciousness. A thought is just a thought which can be changed. The challenge is not allowing ourselves to be taken over by our thoughts. Our thoughts can be helpful or destructive to our wellbeing.

Worrying about something has never changed anything, so stop worrying. Every day we have thousands of thoughts that create the actions that we seemingly perform every day without even thinking about them. Babies have to consciously learn how to walk until it becomes an unconscious action, whereas breathing somehow happens automatically—and yet, even breathing can become a conscious action. Consciously breathing is a great way to relieve stress.

It is believed that the brain is made up of 10 per cent conscious mind and 90 per cent subconscious mind. In the conscious mind we have our short-term memory and it is where we think, plan and analyse. The subconscious or unconscious mind holds our spiritual connection, intuition, long term memory, developmental stages, emotions, feelings, habits, relationship patterns and involuntary body functions. In Sigmund Freud's psychoanalytic theory of personality, the unconscious mind is defined as a reservoir of feelings, thoughts, urges and memories that are outside of conscious awareness. In order to change these feelings, thoughts and urges that no longer serve you, they have to be brought from the unconscious to the conscious mind in order to form new patterns. The unconscious mind can create unhappiness, so try and catch those negative thoughts before they take hold so that you can transform them into positive, supportive thoughts. Maybe we can recreate the open, tolerant, sharing and loving concept created in the hippie era of the 1960s.

This prompts the question: Who am I beyond my thoughts? You are perceived as strange when the way you think is so different to the way others think. Be who you are, as you are. What are the labels that you have believed to be the 'truth'. Your belief system (BS) detector will let you know if things are true for you. Notice what you feel about what has been said. When you start noticing the emotional response to what has been said, then you are better able to notice the difference in feeling and observing emotions.

Are you brave enough to open the gates that have locked us out through our past beliefs? For instance, in some Jewish folklore, Lilith appears as Adam's first wife, who was created at the same time and from the same clay as Adam—compare Genesis 1:27 (this contrasts with Eve, who was created from one of Adam's ribs: Genesis 2:22). Who knew!

11

Be a Good Friend— Notice Anger

'I believe tears are holy, because they show us that the ice of our heart is melting.'
Barbara De Angelis

FRIENDSHIP

'Lots of people want to ride with you in the limo but what you want is someone who will take the bus with you when the limo breaks down.'
Oprah Winfrey

What is true friendship and how do you define a true friend?

For me, a true friend is someone with whom you have a very special connection, a connection that transcends time and place. Real friends love and accept you for who you really are—the good, the bad and the ugly. A good friend is someone who's company you enjoy, is kind, respectful, trustworthy, loyal and is happy to really listen to you. They will laugh with you, support you when you are crying, willing to tell you the truth no matter how hard it is to hear and will stick around when things get tough. Most importantly, they don't judge you, hurt your feelings or deliberately put you down. Overall, both being and having a good friend is great for your wellbeing.

My mother told me when I was young that I was blessed if I had one really good friend. A decade ago, my granddaughter told me that she had over two hundred friends. I asked her how many of those friends she really knew. Her response was, 'All of them.' My granddaughter obviously has a different perspective of what it means to be a friend. Some friends I call acquaintances—they come and go in your life. Other friends you may have known for a long time, since school, and others may have recently entered your life and said, 'I am here for you,' and proved it.

One of the only true choices that we really make in our life is choosing our true friends and yet it is also said that we choose the family we come into before birth to experience a certain life. Social media has set up a whole new and different category of friends. Whilst our social media friends are possibly people that we have met at work, sport, functions or similar interest activities, our only connection with these friends are via cyber space. How well do you really know these friends other than the connection that you made at one point in time? I have had 'friend requests' from people who are friends of friends I don't even know.

The world is filled with so many wonderful people and social media allows us to keep in contact with people all over the world for free. Although I am of the belief that nothing is really free, which is a whole other discussion. Friendships fit into many different categories, intimate friends and/or partners, social friends, family, work or school friends and the social media friends that you never connect with anymore. When I heard someone say with a smile and a laugh, 'I stalked you on Facebook the other day,' I realised that I was definitely in a different era. Being stalked in my younger years was definitely not a laughing matter nor a pleasant experience.

The relationships we have are meant to help us grow and evolve as human beings. True friends are fun and easy to be with, sharing great and often in-depth conversations, who call us on our issues, push us to grow, and support us through this process. These friends are very special people so never underestimate how important true friends really are. We are not meant to be alone, and a good friendship is not one way. Therefore, if you are surrounded by people who do not have a positive mindset, or do not treat you in ways that are loving or respectful, then maybe you need to look for new friends. Never underestimate the amount of influence that our friends and environment can truly have on our lives.

If the friendship is important to you, then appreciate what you have and nurture it. As an analogy to describe the difference between cyber friendships and direct contact friendships, consider your friendship as an apple seed. You put the seed on the table and water it for months. Naturally, if you were to water the seed on the table for a million years, it still wouldn't grow into a tree. But if you put this seed into the ground and watered it, it would become a tree. The potential for greatness in that seed is always there, but the right environment makes all the difference to its growth.

DISTRACTED CONNECTION

Have you ever really been conscious of what you are doing on a daily basis or are you on a Ferris wheel going round and around doing the same thing day in and day out, as if you are in automatic mode? Recently, I have been observing other people especially when they are greeting each other. With the imposed social distancing rules many of the connections between people seem to be superficial and brief. Then on the odd occasion people will actually show genuine connection, with joy on their faces, their body language, and often a hug. Even the way people embrace each other is very different. The only thing that is similar with each embrace is that most people actually turn their hearts away and connect with their right sides.

This way of hugging each other is not a heart-to-heart embrace. Unless I have been misinformed, our hearts are on the left side of our bodies, so why do we turn our hearts away when we are hugging? When I started to really be conscious of what I was automatically doing, I wondered if I was the only one. By watching others, I noticed that what I was doing was not solely my actions. We have become accustomed to people smiling at us, and yet I have often wondered how much real emotion is behind that smile or when someone says, 'I love you,' how much emotion and meaning is behind those words. The word 'love' applies to so many things and is often said in so many ways for many different things.

Authenticity of our words and actions seem to have disappeared and I can even hear my ego questioning what I have just written however in my heart I know this to be true. These days, I am personally trying to be more conscious and authentic with what I say and do. When there is nothing left in this material world, what is left? The gift of this particular time on the planet is knowing that it is not about all the stuff I may have or want, it is the love I have for my family, friends and humanity. This time is really about finding the heart of humanity.

NOTICING YOUR ENERGY

It seems as though there is a never-ending evolution of elections—here, there and everywhere—and the catch-cry is job creation and economic growth.

It has never been more important, than right now, to really look at the choices that we are making for our lives, our families and the lives of those coming after us. Everything that we do impacts something else. What humanity has shown after times of crisis is that we can rise like the phoenix and create a more sustainable world for all. There is a great resistance to the waking up of humanity, or at least to the opening of our eyes to really see what is transpiring, by those forces who are benefiting from this mayhem. Many times, I have wonder if this is reality or part of a movie that I had seen before.

Nikola Tesla, best known for his contribution to the design of the modern alternating current electricity supply, once said, 'If you wish to understand the universe, think of energy, frequency and vibration.'

The universe is comprised of energy. Our body and mind are similar to an antenna transmitting and receiving energy signals from the world around us. How much these energy signals or vibrations impact us personally will depend on our energy sensitivity. We translate these vibrations into thoughts, emotions or actions. When I am feeling down or a lack of energy, all I have to do is listen to some music, go for a walk in nature or dip my toes in the ocean.

In traditional Chinese medicine, *chi* refers to the life force energy that flows in and through our body and any blockages to the flow of 'chi' can create 'dis-ease'. *Feng shui* is a practice that uses the flow of energy to harmonise people and their surrounding environment. In English, *feng shui* literally translates to 'wind-water.' Our body needs both air and water to survive. The waves that you see in the water is actually energy moving through the water creating the waves. Water can produce hydroelectric power and wind is the force that drives turbines which then produces electricity.

The challenge is to free up that life force energy within us. When you find and free up that life force energy that is within all of us, you will be better able to nourish yourself, your creativity, your vitality and enhance your relationships to a much higher level of love and connection. Firstly, you need to find the 'spark' that comes from within.

NOTICING ANGER

Emotional hijacking and coercive control do not just happen within the family. We are emotional beings who are influenced by what the world is mirroring all around us. It does not take much to get an emotional reaction from people at the moment. Our mental health and wellbeing have been severely tested and everybody has their own unique struggles. So many people have found themselves challenged with lockdowns, loss of jobs, constrictions and social distancing which all run against our natural human life-force energy. Then there are the stories and fears that arise when the personality is overrun by an ego that sees everything as a threat to its existence. Add to that the additional challenges of business closures, inability to pay rent or mortgages or just trying to make ends meet. During these times, the support of family and friends is essential. When people are on hyper drive, it does not take much to trigger angry emotions. Whilst the anger may be warranted, the way in which the anger is expressed may not be acceptable or appropriate. The first step to dealing with anger is noticing if it is yours and realising that no one can make you feel anything, if you choose not to engage with it. Anger is a natural emotion, but you can control how you respond to it. When a man is angry at his wife, he will often respond to her in a very different way than when he is angry at his boss.

It is often hard to find the answers to get us over those 'humps' in life. Often, we will look outside of ourselves to find the answers because we want to find that magic bullet, a way to stop the hurt and shut down what we perceive as negative emotions and feelings. What I have learnt is that we will never find the answers to our challenges outside of ourselves. The answers we seek are within and we know what we need to do. Our feelings are our feelings, and they are neither good nor bad, they are just feelings, which are showing up to be healed. Language was designed to express our feelings however it is often hard to notice what we are feeling and find the words to express those feelings.

With this in mind, is it any wonder that most things we see, hear or read in our media and marketing is geared to sway public emotion? Facts do not usually sway public emotion but if the story is full of fear, then people are likely to consume that fear, not necessarily any of the factual information that had been presented. Headlines like, 'You need to know…' make an assumption that I want to know. Wrong.

In 2020, the Premier of Victoria gave a daily update of the number of people that had contracted the virus that day and then the number of people that had died that day and on and on it went for weeks. The fear that this generated and the invasion on our daily lives, mind, body and emotions are impossible to measure. Is it any wonder that more people were reaching out for mental health support during this time? The good part of this time is that many parents, that I have spoken to were actually turning off their television to stop the impact on their children. They had woken up and seen the impact that leaving the television on all day had on their children when they had to be home-schooled. These parents noticed how much their children were impacted emotionally, which created fear and changes in their behaviours. If adults were thrown off course during this time, and imbued with fear, my concern is for the long-term impact on both the children and adults.

What is great is that people are now waking up to what is being presented to them and questioning the validity of the information presented. Although with the amount of information that has been presented, it is hard to know what the truth really is. The validity of anything often depends on your beliefs or who you believe is telling the truth. I remember an advertisement many years ago where a son asked his father, 'Dad why did they build the wall of China?' His father replied, 'To keep the rabbits out.' The next day, the boy stood in front of his class and reported what his father had told him, and he was laughed at by his classmates. I wonder if that boy ever believed his father again. But that was only an advertisement!

PRESENT MOMENT

> *'Yesterday is history. Tomorrow is a mystery. And today? Today is a gift. That's why we call it the present.'*
> **Eleanor Roosevelt**

Being in the present moment involves acknowledging what is going on, what is happening and what you are feeling right here and now. Feeling is the language of our soul and the gift to ourselves is learning to truly acknowledge your feelings and listening to what your soul wants to communicate. It is really hard to even be aware of what is going on in the present moment because we have so many wonderful ways of being distracted or distracting ourselves.

Telepathy is the unspoken language that we speak to one other, a mode of transmitting information without using the usual and familiar sensory channels of communication or physical interaction. Through this form of communication, the truth will be revealed, and it will be extremely difficult to portray things that are untrue. This form of communication creates much more transparency.

It is so important to be conscious of our own emotions. If we lose this connection, we enter a state commonly referred to as 'the living dead' because only dead people don't feel. A lot of our hurt comes from unexpressed feeling, but you need to feel to heal. Therefore, it is so very important to keep our frequency high and be conscious of what our mind and emotions are focused on. What you focus on grows. Simply having a positive mindset when you get up in the morning will change the way you will view the rest of the day. I am an empath and consequently can get emotional very easily. I have noticed that if I can watch a programme or the news as an observer, devoid of any emotion, then I am less likely to have an emotional reaction. However, this is not so easy as it requires present time consciousness. Yes, I cried during the movie when Lassie got hurt.

EXTERNAL FORCES

Part of being a good friend is also knowing the types of things that matter to those you care about both emotionally and physically. The world is filled with manmade mobile, Wi-Fi and other electromagnetic energy and many people have found that this has impacted their health. If we have a strong immune system, then our body knows how to heal itself, however the constant never-ending bombardment of electromagnetic energy all day and night leaves us with no rest for our body and mind. Even if you turn off your own computer, phones and your Wi-Fi, you will still be impacted by what is happening next door or down the street in your neighbourhood. It is just another invisible enemy that is sapping your energy. So, let us hold compassion in these times for ourselves and all of our brothers and sisters.

EDGING GOD OUT

Our EGO has been described as an acronym for 'Edging God Out'. The job of the ego is to protect us from what it perceives as danger to our personal survival whether that is emotional or physical. An egoist is defined as 'one who is completely devoted to his own interests; a selfish person and egoism is defined as 'inordinate concern for one's own welfare and interests; selfishness'. A person who is selfish, concerned only for their own welfare, is a person who is pushing or edging God out of their life. This is contrary to God's will for us.

I have never followed a specific religious belief however I do believe that there is a higher consciousness which I call 'Great Spirit'. During the very challenging situations that have been created as a result of the pandemic, I have found it extremely difficult at times to stay grounded and present. When I had nothing to give, I had absolutely nothing to give, and it took all the emotional strength that I could muster just to get through the day. I was also conscious that I was not alone in the way that I was feeling, so being the very best friend I could was important. Keeping the conversations as positive as possible was also very challenging. A laugh a day was paramount. The only way I could make sense of what was happening was to believe that the universe had a higher purpose for all this madness.

We were being told to go into our rooms and think about what we had done by reflecting on our lives. I know I had stopped actually being consciously grateful for what I had. And I remembered that there was a time when people used to say 'grace' giving thanks for the meal that they were about to eat, and children knelt at the side of their beds at night to pray and give thanks for their day. Now it seems like we have taken everything for granted.

When did we stop being thankful and grateful for what has been provided for us?

Instead, we build more and more walls around ourselves to hopefully keep ourselves 'safe'. Closing the physical borders of our state and country seem to be quite easy to do however our computers, the cyber-borders are now even more susceptible to invasion. Even the firewalls are no longer working. Walls may reduce the symptoms, but they don't necessarily create more security.

12

Looking after the Future

'As a family that supports freedom from government force and open debate, how can we condone government violence, censorship, and compulsory medical procedures which the Nuremberg Charter and numerous international treaties to which we are signatory emphatically outlaw? As human rights advocates, we must ask ourselves the question: At what point does one stop blindly believing government and pharmaceutical officials?'
Robert F. Kennedy, Jr.

POST-PANDEMIC

Inspiring hope for a better post-pandemic future—is 2020 the wake-up call that all of humanity needed? Can we build back better as our politicians are spruiking? Can we have a future that encourages all people, locally and internationally, to create a world that is more sustainable, resilient and inclusive.

This will all depend on the will of the people. Nothing will happen if people are not inspired by the possibility of genuine change intended for the benefit for all of humanity and not the coercive actions of a few for their own personal gain. By removing the blinkers, we can go from silo thinking to big picture thinking. To change the systems that have been created, we need to change the thinking and culture that created them in the first place. You cannot change anything using the same thinking that was used to create it. How do we turn a fearful community into a more sustainable and productive community? Firstly, we need to possess the willingness to look beyond any limitations and transform our fear into more respectful, joyful and abundant lives.

In 2020, Australia suffered droughts, floods, fires and then the pandemic arrived on our shores. Our borders were shut both internally and externally putting a stop to both international and local tourism as well as separating families. The global pandemic did not discriminate. I do not have a crystal ball, but it is clear that the future will never be the same and the impact of the last few years will affect generations to come. I am hopeful that we can all create a new normal which does no harm to anyone or anything and benefits all of humanity on a global level.

DAWN OF A NEW ERA

Like the sunrise and sunset, the future will unfold in its own unique way. Humanity has found its voice, as more and more people speak up and give voice to injustices that are no longer acceptable or tolerable. Many long-held beliefs will be challenged in a revolution of a different kind. Women are speaking out about misogyny, inequality, coercive behaviours, inappropriate language and inappropriate and non-consensual touch or sex.

Many businesses have closed, while others have had to restructure and look at different ways of operating. Part of restructuring meant that employees were required to work from home which meant that large offices were now no longer required. Some operations were scaled down or created with more of an online presence. This required a whole new way of thinking, forcing many businesses to take a long, hard look at the sustainability of their current way of operating.

When borders were shut and restrictions were placed on the movement of people both within Australia and from overseas, it became very obvious as to just how much we are reliant on other people and countries. Many people lost their jobs, others had their hours and income drastically reduced. This situation also highlighted the number of people working on a casual basis which were not covered by the Government support measures.

During this time, farmers, who had previously relied on backpackers and seasonal workers from the Islands to pick their produce, found it difficult to get their seasonal labour force. Sheep farmers also found it difficult to find enough Australian shearers when New Zealand shearers were locked out. Undocumented workers were also highlighted as part of the workforce that have been used on farms. With so much happening at once many people's lives were turned upside down creating waves of emotion which tested people's ability to cope. The mental health service providers have reported a huge increase in people requiring support, especially in relation to family violence. Whilst many people sought help during these challenging times, others avoided or suppressed their emotions. Is it any wonder that the sale of liquor exploded during this time?

Only time will reveal the long-term impacts, like a pressure cooker or volcano slowly simmering, waiting to erupt. What is really happening behind the closed doors of homes, businesses and governments? On the reverse, other people have funnelled and redirected their newfound energy and through the use of their innate skills they have created new and innovative businesses. The greatest thing that this amazing time in history has demonstrated to us is the variance in coping mechanisms.

While some people have found it difficult others have enjoyed the new enthusiasm and inspiration that they have found with work and family.

This time in history has given us all the opportunity to take a good hard look at our life and given us the chance to recalibrate. We all have the free will to choose, and if you always do what you have always done then things will never change. Changing from constantly doing to being, by taking the time to be in the present moment, right now, and to be still. When you are still you can observe and notice what you are feeling. Constantly being on that Ferris wheel, going around and around doing the same thing day in, day out, there is no opportunity to create something different for your life.

FEAR

> *'People don't fake depression … they fake being okay. Remember that. Be kind.'*
> **Robin Williams**

Fear is a natural reaction that serves the biological function of keeping you safe. Your instincts tell you when something is not right. Fear prompts you to be aware of danger however if there is no danger imminent then you need to look for the cause of the fear and figure out what you can do to change the situation that is generating the fear. Is this fear real and warranted?

FEAR can be an acronym for 'False Evidence Appearing Real'. People who have been traumatised and abused are often in a heightened state of alert, constantly on the look out for the abuser. Victims of family or institutional abuse understand this trauma responses only too well however constantly being in a fight, flight or freeze state will not serve you or your health. Living in a state of constant fear impacts your ability to make clear and logical decisions.

Instead of feeling afraid, use this energy, or lack of energy, to motivate you. Get off the merry-go-round and start by focusing on what you want to create. The gift is to find different ways to channel and focus your fearful emotions to enhance your life rather than spiralling further down the black hole. This can be easier said than done and depends on how far down you are at this point in time. Sometimes all you can do is get up out of bed and put one foot in front of the other. Listen to music, go for a walk in nature, watch birds or do anything that makes you smile. Focusing on at least three things that you are grateful for every single day can change your mood. For me, sunshine and music have always been a great source of joy, and when I was at my lowest, having my beautiful dog to care for gave me a reason to live.

Beyond the next moment is the future. The future starts with reclaiming your power. The only thing that you can change is what you do, so speak up and demand respect by saying 'no' to what is no longer serving your highest good. At this time, that may be saying 'no' to going back to a job where you don't feel that you get the respect and appreciation you deserve. Say 'no' to a lifestyle of increasing debt. How can you create a safe and secure future for you and your loved ones? Learn to live simply to simply live.

Can we save the world? No. Can we change what we do and influence what happens in the future? Definitely. This happens one person at a time starting with you and me. There is a saying that 'you can lead a horse to water, but you can't make it drink.' What I hope to achieve is give you another perspective, another way of looking at what is happening in the world. The next step is looking beyond what has been to what will be in the future. One thing that business owners know for sure is that you have to be prepared to change and adapt to what is happening. For instance, what are we doing to people and their jobs when people are being replaced by robots and everything is being computerised? What value does that place on people and the incredible contribution that they make to our communities?

IN CHANGING TIMES

> *'There is no such thing as away. When you throw something away, it must go somewhere.'*
> **Annie Leonard**

In a race to discover the difference between self-destruction and self-understanding, we find the truth for ourselves and acknowledge that the human race is intrinsically good. Human consciousness has been disconnected from our 'divine source' for far too long, resulting in our current human condition. Similarly, we have been unjustly condemned for being bad for far too long, and this requires healing. When we can all believe that we are intrinsically good, caring, loving and wonderful, then we can embrace all of ourselves with love and acceptance.

I wonder if the virus that has wreaked so much havoc, realised that it had so much power to influence and reshape the lives of so many people. For many years climate activists have been concerned about the trajectory of the health of our planet, the extinction of animals and the health of people due to the pollution that has been created on our planet. What has amazed me is just how quickly people can change when required, so there is hope. The real craziness is that so much damage has been created on earth and now we are going to mars. Why? Is it so that the people on earth will have somewhere to go when we have destroyed our beautiful planet?

Whilst this time has been challenging, it has also given me hope. Many people actually stopped and became aware of what they were doing in their own lives. Sustainability has become a personal issue, not just a problem for someone else to solve—the issue is here and now. Many people began to question what they were doing in their own lives and how they could do things differently.

In the words of Lynne Twist, veteran global activist and fundraiser and the author of *The Soul of Money*:

> *'People want to know what to do, and I think that's a good question too. But a more profound question and a more powerful question is who do we need to be? And I think who we need to be are people who know that the decisions and choices we make now impact the future of life for the next hundred years. Everybody alive today has a role to play. You don't have a big role and you don't have a small role, you just have your role. And if you play it, then your life will really have a kind of meaning that you've dreamt of.'*

Whilst Twist only mentioned the next hundred years, I would not put any time limit on achieving sustainability for all of humanity. It is our responsibility to deal with what we have created, not bury or throw it away for someone else to deal with in future. That is grossly irresponsible. If you created the mess, you must clean it up. In our modern world, we create so much rubbish, so what would you do differently if your rubbish was not taken away?

NEXT GENERATION

How prepared is the next generation to tackle the biggest challenges facing the future of our planet? Teachers ranked the following skills and attributes required for future generations in order of their importance: STEM (Science, Technology, Engineering and Mathematics), problem solving and critical thinking, creativity and innovation, compassion, grit (determination, resilience, perseverance), emotional intelligence and trade skills.

Children can develop many of these key skills by learning outdoors, both during and outside of school hours, so providing opportunities for outdoor learning is a critical priority for parents, teachers and the wider community. Sadly, children have lost touch with nature in a way that has never been experienced before. Previously three out of four adults played outdoors more often than indoors when they were young, compared to one in ten children today. Toddlers now use digital devices from an early age, parents work long hours and there are heightened fears of child safety and pressure to engage in extracurricular activities, which all limit the amount of time children spend in nature.

Children who have positive relationships, good problem-solving skills, grit and enhanced emotional intelligence skills will be happier, healthier and more successful in the future. Future generations will also need to learn how to persist through hardships and setbacks with the support of parents and carers, schools and teachers, and society as a whole. Most of all, I feel that it is really important to get reconnected to the natural world instead of the sterile four walls of classrooms and homes. The recent inclusion of outdoor learning in the Australian curriculum is a leap forward for future nature-based experiences within the school day. Simple activities, like riding bikes, going for a bush walk, taking homework or mealtime outside or joining organised community activities, can have a significant impact on a child's connection to nature. It is all about creating a learning environment that is much more engaging.

Many years ago, I read a story of a rich dad and his wise son. This gives me hope for the future.

Rich Dad and His Wise Son
One day, a rich dad took his son on a trip to show him how poor people lived.

They spent time on the farm of a poor family.

On the way home, Dad asked his son;

How poor they are? What did you learn from this trip?

His Son said…

We have one dog, they have four of them.

We have a pool, they have a river.

We have tube-lights at night, they have stars.

We buy food, they grow their food.

We have walls to protect us, they have friends.

We have television, they spend time with family and relatives.

Then he added:

Thanks, Dad, for showing me how poor we are!

The moral of the story is that it's not about money, or clothes, or gadgets, or cars, or a big house. It's simplicity, love, compassion, friendships, values, and family that make our lives rich.

How do you perceive your life? Is money all that matters to you? Or is it love that inspires you every single moment to be a better human being?

DO NO HARM

'Let food be thy medicine and medicine be thy food.'
Hippocrates

The Hippocratic Oath is an oath of ethics, historically taken by physicians. It is one of the most widely known of all Greek medical texts. In its original form, it requires a new physician to swear, by a number of healing gods, to uphold specific ethical standards.

The original oath still resonates, particularly the phrase, 'I will utterly reject harm and mischief,' which is commonly misquoted as, 'First, do no harm.' For me, that fits perfectly with not over-diagnosing, not over-treating, and sharing the decision-making.

Hippocratic Oath: Original Version
'I swear by Apollo Healer, by Asclepius, by Hygieia, by Panacea, and by all the gods and goddesses, making them my witnesses, that I will carry out, according to my ability and judgement, this oath and this indenture.

To hold my teacher in this art equal to my own parents; to make him partner in my livelihood; when he is in need of money to share mine with him; to consider his family as my own brothers, and to teach them this art, if they want to learn it, without fee or indenture; to impart precept, oral instruction, and all other instruction to my own sons, the sons of my teacher, and to indentured pupils who have taken the Healer's oath, but to nobody else.

I will use those dietary regimens which will benefit my patients according to my greatest ability and judgement, and I will do no harm or injustice to them. Neither will I administer a poison to anybody when asked to do so, nor will I suggest such a course. Similarly I will not give to a woman a pessary to cause abortion. But I will keep pure and holy both my life and my art. I will not use the knife, not even, verily, on sufferers from stone, but I will give place to such as are craftsmen therein.

Into whatsoever houses I enter, I will enter to help the sick, and I will abstain from all intentional wrong-doing and harm, especially from abusing the bodies of man or woman, bond or free. And whatsoever I shall see or hear in the course of my profession, as well as outside my profession in my intercourse with men, if it be what should not be published abroad, I will never divulge, holding such things to be holy secrets.

Now if I carry out this oath, and break it not, may I gain for ever reputation among all men for my life and for my art; but if I break it and forswear myself, may the opposite befall me.'

Translation by W.H.S. Jones.

Hippocratic Oath: Classical Version
'I will neither give a deadly drug to anybody who asked for it, nor will I make a suggestion to this effect. Similarly, I will not give to a woman an abortive remedy. In purity and holiness, I will guard my life and my art.'

My vision for humanity and Mother Earth is to 'do no harm' to anyone or anything by standing together and leaving no one out. This relates to all areas of our lives starting with the way we think and speak about ourselves and others. We never know how our words, actions or inaction will impact upon those around us. Be very conscious of what you are doing, in your work and your daily life as sometimes we just follow the crowd as if in a daze. Walk lightly on Mother Earth and respect and appreciate her as she has always taken care of our forebears, our generation and hopefully future generations. Using ancient wisdom, they knew that the earth has everything that we need to heal us with herbs, plants, essential oils, and all other natural things including clean air and water. What we need to do is tune into that ancient wisdom or at least listen to those that can.

When I think about information technology and the phones on steroids, it feels like the gate has been opened and the horse has bolted.

'As a society we fear the impact of global warming on our planet, as we try and mitigate the many causes. Have we even considered the impact of our mobile phones, phone towers, satellites and the WiFi radiation.'
Arthur Firstenberg

The executive summary produced by the 5G Space Appeal, which you can view at https://www.5gspaceappeal.org/the-appeal, reads:

'Telecommunications companies worldwide, with the support of governments, are poised within the next two years to roll out the fifth-generation wireless network (5G). This is set to deliver what is acknowledged to be unprecedented societal change on a global scale. We will have 'smart' homes, 'smart' businesses, 'smart' highways, 'smart' cities and self-driving cars. Virtually everything we own and buy, from refrigerators and washing machines to milk cartons, hairbrushes and infants' diapers, will contain antennas and microchips and will be connected wirelessly to the Internet. Every person on Earth will have instant access to super-high-speed, low- latency wireless communications from any point on the planet, even in rain forests, mid-ocean and the Antarctic.

What is not widely acknowledged is that this will also result in unprecedented environmental change on a global scale. The planned density of radio frequency transmitters is impossible to envisage. In addition to millions of new 5G base stations on Earth and 20,000 new satellites in space, 200 billion transmitting objects, according to estimates, will be part of the Internet of Things by 2020, and one trillion objects a few years later. Commercial 5G at lower frequencies and slower speeds was deployed in Qatar, Finland and Estonia in mid-2018. The roll out of 5G at extremely high (millimetre wave) frequencies is planned to begin at the end of 2018.

Despite widespread denial, the evidence that radio frequency (RF) radiation is harmful to life is already overwhelming. The accumulated clinical evidence of sick and injured human beings, experimental evidence of damage to DNA, cells and organ systems in a wide variety of plants and animals, and epidemiological evidence that the major diseases of modern civilisation— cancer, heart disease and diabetes—are in large part caused by electromagnetic pollution, forms a literature base of well over 10,000 peer-reviewed studies.

If the telecommunications industry's plans for 5G to come to fruition, no person, no animal, no bird, no insect and no plant on Earth will be able to avoid exposure, 24 hours a day, 365 days a year, to levels of RF radiation that are tens to hundreds of times greater than what exists today, without any possibility of escape anywhere on the planet. These 5G plans threaten to provoke serious, irreversible effects on humans and permanent damage to all of the Earth's ecosystems.

Immediate measures must be taken to protect humanity and the environment, in accordance with ethical imperatives and international agreements.'

PRIVACY VS MAKING OUR WORLD SAFER

On 22 October 1986, the Honourable Neil Blewett MP Minister for Health proposed the Australia Card Bill. The proposal for this bill was released at the Taxation Summit in 1985 and abandoned in 1987. The main reason given for the introduction of the Australia Card was to reduce taxation, Social Security fraud and detect illegal immigrants. At the time, the idea of having the Australia Card created a great uproar in the community with many people demonstrating at the possibility of the loss of their personal freedoms. In reality, we already had the

Medicare card which gave you a personal number, and then in 1988, the Tax File Number was introduced.

It was recently reported that we now have facial recognition. In January 2020, the ABC reported: 'Clearview AI was founded by Australian Hoan Ton-That and sells facial recognition technology to police around the world.' Facial recognition is going to change the relationship between the people who are watching and the people who are being watched.

So much for our privacy. Fast forward to 2020, we have the electronic track and tracing app, a location device on mobiles and an electronic corona virus QR code was created. In March 2021 there was an article in the Telegraph, *How Boris Johnson went from threatening to eat his ID card to opening door to pub Covid passports*. Many people in the 1980s were assured that there would never be an ID card. The ID passport for a virus is an ID card of another name and under another guise. Now is everyone good to go.

In many ways, I concede that technology is a great tool, and we have come a long way from the times of the paper scroll, however technology has created a time of information overload. Information about anything or anyone can be posted anywhere, anytime via a computer. These days it seems like everyone has an opinion, and yes, that includes me, however I admit that I don't know everything about everything.

UNINTENDED CONSEQUENCES

With all of the benefits technology provides, there are downsides. It is now easier to find someone with the tracking and tracing app making stalking much more prevalent and so much easier these days. The women who have experienced domestic violence are way more concerned about the way technology has impacted their private lives.

Before social media, stalking required a physical action, whereas now our emails, Facebook and other social media platforms have made it much easier for stalkers to be more covert and follow every move of their victim. Privacy has gone out the window. In Australia, privacy legislation requires many businesses to protect the personal information that they stored on behalf of their client. Has this now become obsolete?

Listening to a television programme called *Landline*, I was informed of the unintended consequences of lobbyists against the use of animal hides. Because of these animal protection lobbyists, our shoes are now rarely made from leather. Shoes that were once made from natural products, like animal hides from already deceased animals, are now being made from petrochemicals and other artificial means. In some ways, I feel that if an animal is killed then at least respect all of what this animal has given and don't waste any part of it.

When I went to Kenya and visited a Maasai village I noted just how much care and protection they gave their animals. Every animal was precious and all parts were used, and there was not the mass slaughter we have in our western world. Also, Maasai children under ten years of age were not fed meat. Like most indigenous cultures, the Maasai respect nature and nature looks after them. In African philosophy the word 'ubuntu' means 'I am because you are' being the self through others. Ubuntu is that nebulous concept of common humanity, oneness, you and me both.

In so many ways, our society is blessed and for many people they don't even want to acknowledge that some things are not the way that they believe them to be. Years ago, I watched the film *WALL-E*, which prompted me to wonder if this is the world that I would want our children, grandchildren and beyond to inherit.

Money does nothing. People do everything.

'When I welcome you—when our Aunties and Uncles welcome you—we are welcoming you to a place. But we're actually welcoming you to the intimate relationship we have to that place. We're also welcoming you to our kin. We're welcoming you to the significant relationships we have with the people of our place. We're welcoming you to our roles, responsibilities and obligations, that keep us connected and bound through these people, to our place.'
Yuin man - Jade Kennedy

Acknowledgement to Country

I see the connection of Aboriginal people and their history with the land, place and culture and I acknowledge and pay respect to the Traditional Custodians and Elders right across this beautiful country. I thank them for allowing me to live, work and visit their spiritual lands. I acknowledge my ancestors and old people for their continuous guidance and protection as I go about my work educating and inspiring people to believe in themselves and follow their dreams.

SERENITY PRAYER

GOD grant me the

SERENITY to accept the things I cannot change,

COURAGE to change the things I can and the

WISDOM to know the difference.

Declaration for Earth— Revoking Unconscious Consent

We, the people of Earth, do not give you, the invisible dark forces, beings, and entities, permission to control us in any form imaginable.

We, the people, do not give you permission to make us war against each other, to poison our food and water supplies, to poison us with chemicals that harm the human body, the animals and the environment.

We, the people, do not give you permission to hold our sovereignty from us or to govern us through heads of state that profit from the people energetically, physically, mentally, emotionally, spiritually and any other forms of vampirism.

We, the people, now take our planet Earth back under our control for the betterment of all citizens on the planet, and demand you, the dark forces which are part of the invisible, to leave this planet with immediate effect.

References

Rich Dad, Poor Dad, Robert T Kiyosaki

You Can Heal Your Life, Louise Hay

Ageless Body, Timeless Mind, Deepak Chopra

The Soul of Money: Transforming Your Relationship with Money and Life, Lynne Twist

Women's Body, Women's Wisdom: Creating Physical and Emotional Health and Healing, Christiane Northrup MD

The Speed of Trust: The One Thing That Changes Everything, Stephen M R Covey

Smart Trust: Creating Prosperity, Energy and Joy in a Low Trust World, Stephen M.R. Covey, Greg Link, Rebecca R. Merrill

Plague of Corruption: Restoring Faith in the Promise of Science, Dr Judy Mikovits & Kent Heckenlively, JD

The Invisible Rainbow: A History of Electricity and Life, Arthur Firstenberg

WorkPlace Plus. *What Are the Must Have Policies for Our Employee Manual?* 3 March 2021. https://www.workplaceplus.com.au/post/what-are-the-must-have-policies-for-our-employee-manual

ABS. https://www.abs.gov.au/ausstats/abs

Country Economy, *https://countryeconomy.com/national-debt/australia*

Speaker Bio

Petra is an advocate and mentor who, in order to be the change she wanted to see in the world, realised helping others was easier than helping herself. This once unofficial tax collector, council candidate, entrepreneur, employee and humanitarian has seen so much change in her life, health and business, that many things now feel alien.

With over 50-plus years of work and life experiences, writing the book '50 Shades of Black and White – An Idealist's Reflections,' highlighted her unique and individualistic way of thinking. Petra has often been told that she should go into politics however she decided to write a book instead.

Our language seems to be constantly changing and sometimes the meaning of words are lost in translation. Words such as 'choice' are being portrayed in a 'coercive controlling' way and 'inclusion' feels like 'exclusion.' Even 'breast feeding' has now been called 'chest feeding.' Is 'consent' about giving permission, valuing bodily sovereignty and allowing self expression? What do words really mean and more importantly what do they mean to you?

Really understanding each other, and the laws of the land, seem to have become more and more complicated especially when the rules are constantly changing. Is it any wonder that life sometimes feels out of control!

> *'The definition of Insanity is doing the same thing over and over and expecting a different result.'*
> **Albert Einstein**

Petra is available to speak to various groups on the following topics:

BUSINESS AND WORK
- Have computers taken over our lives or given us more freedoms?
- Is the life force energy of humanity being blocked, through social distancing and isolation, creating dis-ease and disharmony between the people and their surroundings.
- Changing the way business is done can change so many other things?
- Does local control in business engender more honesty and transparency?

LIFE
- Why is it that children can no longer grow up or play without adult supervision?
- Have we become a society of fear?
- How do we feel and acknowledge our fear and still love and trust one another?
- Did you know that Australian citizens have no Bill Of Rights?
- How do we rebuild the genuine Australian spirit of mate-ship?
- Are our freedoms and choices slowly being diminished, often without anyone being aware of what is actually happened?
- Did we really have any freedoms in the first place and do we need to have a revolution to regain lost freedoms?

- What are the verbal and written contracts that we have with each other?
- Can people still understand each other with the continued change of language?
- Does our education need to be expanded from reading, writing and arithmetic to include respect, rights, responsibility and reciprocity?
- Is reciprocity really a social norm of responding to a positive action with another positive action, rewarding kind actions, or something else?

HEALTH

- Learn the art of focused breathing, a simple practice that can reduce stress.
- Learn how to reconnect to your soul and ask your soul what it wants from you. Are you living or just existing? Who has the power in your life?
- Separate your 'needs' from your 'wants' in order to live a simpler life.
- Having a digital presence should not be a requirement to your existence. Mobile phones and computers are tools that can enhance and harm your life. Too long the truth of harmful products have been 'hidden' and the only benefits 'proclaimed.' This used to be unlawful. Remembering that not everyone is, or wants to be, attached to their mobile phone.

YOU CAN CONTACT PETRA AT
petrabethechange@gmail.com

'You can speak with spiritual eloquence, pray in public, and maintain a holy appearance…but it is your behaviour that will reveal your true character.'
Dr Steve Maraboli

About the Author

About the Author

Petra is someone who cares about social justice, the environment and the type of future that her grandchildren, great-grandchildren and generations after will inherit. As a catalyst for change and a citizen educator who challenges peoples' thinking, Petra's hope is that, in reading her book, her reflections will be dispersed and sown like seeds on fertile ground.

As Petra has been known to be political and outspoken, she acknowledges and understands the frustration in feeling unheard or that others do not care about the issues she is passionate about. In writing this book, she wishes to share her unique journey and champion the cause of leaving no one behind in this fast-paced world. This is her innovative way of communicating in the hope of inspiring you and those around you to awaken and open up to a different way of thinking.

Petra is very grateful to her parents for migrating to Australia in the 1950s, as this has allowed her to live and raise her family in what she considers to be the best country in the world.

> *Yesterday I was clever, so I wanted to change the world. Today I am wise, so I am changing myself.*
> **Rumi**